TEACH JUSTICE & BELONGING

A JOURNEY FOR
EDUCATORS & PARENTS

TEHIA STARKER GLASS, Ph.D.
LUCRETIA CARTER BERRY, Ph.D.

JB JOSSEY-BASS™
A Wiley Brand

Jossey-Bass
A Wiley Imprint
111 River St, Hoboken, NJ 07030
www.josseybass.com

Library of Congress Cataloging-in-Publication Data

Names: Glass, Tehia Starker, author. | Berry, Lucretia Carter, author.
Title: Teaching for justice & belonging : a journey for educators & parents
 / Tehia Starker Glass, Lucretia Carter Berry
Description: [San Francisco] : Jossey-Bass, [2022] | Includes
 bibliographical references and index.
Identifiers: LCCN 2022023199 (print) | LCCN 2022023200 (ebook) | ISBN
 9781119834328 (paperback) | ISBN 9781119834373 (adobe pdf) | ISBN
 9781119834359 (epub)
Subjects: LCSH: Social justice—Study and teaching. | Anti-racism—Study
 and teaching.
Classification: LCC LC192.2 .G53 2022 (print) | LCC LC192.2 (ebook) | DDC
 370.11/5—dc23/eng/20220609
LC record available at https://lccn.loc.gov/2022023199
LC ebook record available at https://lccn.loc.gov/2022023200

Cover Design: Wiley
Cover Image: © CPD-Lab/Getty Images

SKY10035177_071122

For our ancestors and parents, who walked us from their past

For our children, who are guiding us to their future

Contents

About the Authors

Tehia Starker Glass, PhD (pronounced Tee-ah; she/her/hers) is the Cato College of Education Director of diversity and inclusion and award-winning Associate Professor of Educational Psychology and Elementary Education in the Department of Reading and Elementary Education at the University of North Carolina (UNC) Charlotte. Dr. Glass is also the Inclusive Excellence Executive Fellow for faculty development in the Office of Diversity and Inclusion at UNC Charlotte. She is a Student Experience Research Network (SERN) fellow and uses her research and expertise to inform education policy. Her research and publications include preparing preservice and in-service teachers' culturally responsive teaching self-efficacy, culturally responsive teaching in teacher education, racial identity development, anti-racism curriculum development, and exploring how caregivers and teachers discuss race with children. She is a proud graduate of Bethune-Cookman University (BS in elementary education), University of Northern Iowa (MA in educational technology), and University of Nebraska–Lincoln (PhD in educational psychology).

Dr. Glass is a former elementary school teacher who now consults nationally with educators, schools, districts, companies, and organizations to be more anti-racism oriented. She is a TED speaker (Cultivating Seeds of Curiosity), and educational advisor and certified trainer with Brownicity. She cofounded and is the co-director of the Anti-Racism Graduate Certificate Program at UNC Charlotte. She lives in the Charlotte area with her partner and two boys.

Lucretia Carter Berry, PhD (she/her/hers) is founder and president of Brownicity, an agency committed to making important, scholarly informed, antiracism education accessible, and director of its online membership platform. With the tagline *Many Hues, One Humanity*, Brownicity's mission is to foster education designed to inspire a culture of justice and true belonging for all.

Berry earned her PhD in curriculum and instruction and MA in English from Iowa State University and her BA from South Carolina State University. A former college professor, Berry's research, experience, and accomplishments lie at the intersections of curriculum and instruction, multicultural and antiracism education, and instructional technology. She contributed to the design of and was an instructor for the *Carver Academy Multicultural Learning Communities Project* (Iowa State University), which was nationally recognized for increasing the retention rate for underrepresented students. A leader in her field, Berry was the vice president of the Equity and Social Justice Committee for Society of Information Technology in Teacher Education (SITE). She served on the steering committee for the Social Justice and Digital Equity Pre-conference Symposium, where she had the privilege of working with colleagues from around the world to grant the Outstanding Service to Digital Equity Award.

As a wife in an interracial marriage and mom of three multiethnic children, Berry brings her personal and professional experience to the public sector, where she is passionate about serving children and their adult decision-makers. In 2015, she synthesized a multitude of consultations with children, parents, teachers, and leaders to launch a grassroots education agency, Brownicity. Berry designed curricula and other learning experiences to onboard and support learners of all ages by partnering with individuals, churches, schools, and companies.

Berry designed Brownicity's flagship course and study guide, *What LIES Between Us—Fostering First Steps Toward Racial Healing* (2016), and authored *Hues of You—An Activity Book for Learning About the Skin You Are In* (2022). She is a TED speaker (*Children will light up the world if we don't keep them in the dark*), a course designer, a curriculum specialist for Community School of Davidson (NC), and a contributor for (In)courage.me, a DaySpring online community.

Berry and her husband, Nathan, have three daughters and two Aussiedoodles, and live in the Charlotte, NC area.

Acknowledgments

This work is not only dedicated to but also made possible by the thousands of children, families, educators, schools, leaders, churches, companies, and communities who believe in the future that we see and have aligned themselves with the vision to manifest justice and belonging for all. We are extra appreciative of those who lent their voices and stories to these pages to offer our readers additional support and encouragement—especially those from our Brownicity Team, who have been collectively and actively forging a way forward since 2015. We must acknowledge and express gratitude to our parents, who were our first teachers and who taught us to navigate, with style and grace, a society that often devalues its Black daughters.

To our husbands and children: without your consistent support, we would not have been able to commit to and persist in this journey.

And we are especially grateful to the colleagues, friends, and our crew who honor us by choosing to love, learn, and lead with us.

CHAPTER 1
Welcome to Our Garden

A garden requires patient labor and attention. Plants do not grow merely to satisfy ambitions or to fulfill good intentions. They thrive because someone expended effort on them.
—Liberty Hyde Bailey, Country Life in America

Welcome to our garden.

We are Tehia Starker Glass and Lucretia Carter Berry. In 2016, we were e-introduced to each other by a mutual colleague who, due to our commitment to antiracism, children, and the adults who care for them, believed that we could potentially make a great team. We met up at Panera for lunch and have been cultivating a friendship and scholarship ever since. We have so much in common. We both earned our undergraduate degrees from HBCUs (historically Black colleges and universities). We earned our graduate degrees from HWI's (historically White institutions) in the Midwest. We earned our doctorates in education before we married our extroverted husbands. We. Are. Introverts. And we both taught in classrooms before we had our own children.

Our lunchtime meetup was somewhat out of the ordinary. We arrived with the expectation of learning more about each other, to test the waters. However, as we shared our personal stories, our hearts, and our motivation for supporting educators and parents, we felt as if we had already known each other for years. Before our lunch was over, we had forged our superpowers. We assigned each other projects, responsibilities, and goal dates. We trusted each other!

As scholars, creatives, advocates, and mothers, we are deeply rooted and invested in cultivating a just and belonging culture in our homes, classrooms, and communities. In fact, we've had the privilege of embodying this practice for years. It has been and continues to be a journey for which the destination is secondary. We've experienced clear pathways (our first meeting), winding roads (the bureaucracy that tends to value performance over embodied transformative practice), and a few potholes (some well-intentioned folks who simply can't connect to the vision). But mostly, our journey has afforded us the opportunity to support parents and teachers— preservice and in-service—as they begin to navigate the terrain of truly caring for the children in their spaces.

The order of the words *justice* and *belonging* is intentional. We have observed that while the idea of belonging is widely accepted and celebrated, the idea of a just home, classroom, or learning environment remains somewhat elusive and abstract. However, we understand that where justice is prioritized, belonging exists and persists.

We are witnessing masses of teachers, teacher leaders, college professors, and parents awaken to the value of cultivating justice and belonging in classrooms, homes, and communities. You are probably one of them. We sincerely appreciate your courageous curiosity and want to offer you support, wisdom, and guidance for your journey. As a parent, educator, or teacher-leader, you are positioned and advantaged to strategically foster learning that inspires a culture of true belonging, liberation, and justice for all.

Dear Parents and Educators,

Allow us to offer you support as you shift your teaching, curricula, instruction, pedagogy, and policies to center antibias and antiracism practices. We will demonstrate how to explore personal and collective racial identities to learn more about self and others. So that you can learn from practical experiences, we share real stories and testimonials from parents and teachers. Because the fear of messing up is real and has paralyzed some people on this journey, we want to help you shift from reservation to results-oriented action. And of course, we share resources and practices for a healthy journey. Essentially, amid these pages we disclose a growth map for a healthy antibias, antiracism journey.

We understand that you want to raise racially literate children and have classrooms and schools that reflect the just, creative, life-giving, hope-filled, connected community that we long for and know is possible. That's why we wrote this book for those who are newer to understanding how race/ism operates in predominantly White schools, and in schools where the population is majority students of color. We want all students—students of color and White students—to have a healthy awareness of self in relation to a racial, ethnic, and cultural group membership and to understand the social and political implications of their racial and ethnic identity. This book is also for parents, caregivers, and guardians who want to help foster a healthy racial and ethnic identity for themselves and the children for whom they are responsible.

In these pages, we discuss our own experiences in raising racially aware children and teaching adults to become racially literate inside and outside of schools to position themselves to create justice and belonging. Yolanda Sealy-Ruiz and the National Council of Teachers of English (2021) defines racial literacy as "a skill and practice by which individuals can probe the existence of racism and examine the effects of race and institutionalized systems on their experiences and representation in US society. Students who have this skill can discuss the implications of race and American racism in constructive ways." Similar to language literacy or mathematical literacy, racial literacy affords fluency in helpful dialogue, vision casting, and solutions. Racially literate parents and teachers are able see and dismantle obstacles embedded by racism—institutional, structural, interpersonal, and internalized—that impede our children's potential and aspirations.

Before We Begin

We want to set you up for success. We have witnessed many people forfeit themselves, stall, and even retreat due to disappointments they encounter along the way. Metaphorically speaking, journeys—especially lifelong ones—are wrought with detours, delays, and disappointments. And this journey is no different. We've observed that the most injurious disappointments are contrived by unmet or unrealistic expectations. Cultivating homes, classrooms, and communities for justice and belonging requires a commitment to a steady process—one that demands our informed intention, our full attention, and our greatest engagement.

So that you experience more victories than defeats, we list some common misunderstandings and missteps we've observed along with our recommendations for establishing realistic expectations and an informed intention.

1. ***I simply need to sprinkle a few diverse books, videos, websites, and lessons about Black, Indigenous, Asian, and Latinx people into my curriculum.*** Diversifying content is essential, but it does not address or change the root structure that excluded the diversity in the first place. Including diverse books and lessons should be consequential instead of peripheral. Simply adding diverse books and lessons is performative. For example, if you want a multifruit tree, would you glue apples and oranges to a lemon tree? No. You would plant a multifruit tree seed and help it grow.

   Cultivating justice and belonging must be an embodiment or expression of its core constitution rather than simply tacked on or completed. Think about how over time laws and policies have been amended to reflect justice, but society has been slow to shift. For example, though the Supreme Court banned school segregation in 1954, it took another 10 years to implement desegregation, and even now schools remain heavily segregated by race and ethnicity. The roots of segregation continue to produce its fruit. Episodes 562 and 563 of the podcast *This American Life* and the podcast series *Nice White Parents* examine the current consequences of racial and economic inequalities derived from school segregation and desegregation.

   Antiracism is a journey that requires heart work, which we share more about in Chapter 3. At some point along the way, performative actions falter and revert to their origins. Performance is not sustainable. The lemon tree will continue to grow lemons, while the apples and oranges—unrooted— fall aside. No one can afford or deserves a performance.

Trying to be someone other than yourself is exhausting and counterintuitive to the work of antiracism.

2. ***I will focus only on my family or classroom***. We've heard only a few people actually say this out loud, but we've observed many parents and schools attempt to do this work in factions or as a solo project. We know it may feel easier to go at it alone, but as the African proverb says, "If you want to go fast, go alone. If you want to go far, go together."

It is not only beneficial to you but also imperative to our children that we work together in community. Think about it: If you are the only one in your house or school on a growth journey, you will lack support, feel isolated, and may experience frustration. This work cannot be done in a vacuum. You begin this work first on yourself, which takes a while, but you must also involve the circles of people who are a part of your world. Think about the people with whom you work, spend time, and interact daily. The people you are around form a mirror of yourself. Begin in your home with a partner or children. Then extend the work into the workspace with colleagues, students, administrators, and so on. Ultimately, you don't operate in the world alone, and you cannot do this work alone.

3. ***I am a White person who does not have permission or credibility to do this work. I must rely on BIPOC, especially Black people, to teach me how to do this.*** BIPOC is an acronym for Black, Indigenous, (and) People of Color used to acknowledge that not all people of color face racial injustice in the same way. For example, Black and Indigenous Americans are more severely impacted by systemic racial injustices than Asians and White-appearing Latinx. Nevertheless, there is a false pretense that only BIPOC—especially Black people—can be or are naturally qualified to teach for justice and belonging.

We do not know where this idea originated, but this fallacy sets us up for failure. BIPOC didn't create the issues that exist in our world due to racism, and BIPOC cannot bear the burden of repair. We should not and cannot rely on BIPOC to do all the work. White people must pull their weight as well. We all have been racialized, and therefore we all need to examine how this socialization has propagated disconnection, injustice, and inequities. Just because someone is racialized as White does not mean they are incapable of becoming racially literate and engaging in constructive problem-solving. White people are not automatically disqualified. Becoming antiracist to foster justice and belonging in schools, homes, and communities is attainable by *anyone* who remains committed to the journey.

According to the National Center for Educational Statistics (2020), about 80 percent of public school teachers are White, and the remaining 20 percent are teachers of color. It cannot be expected that 20 percent of teachers will bear 100 percent of the load. White teachers can take on the responsibility, embody antiracism, and create just and belonging schools and classrooms. However, we encourage White parents and educators to value and learn from BIPOC antiracists. One of our colleagues who is White told us that when she began her antiracism journey, she skipped over all the resources by BIPOC to find books written by White authors. Fortunately, she realized her error right away. By overlooking BIPOC voices, she unconsciously prioritized comfort and familiarity. She valued what White authors had to say about racial injustice over BIPOC perspectives. While you should not expect BIPOC to do all the work by themselves, you should definitely value and prioritize our work.

4. ***Antiracism centers Black people. I am a person of color who is not Black, so antiracism excludes me.*** The toxicity of racism has impacted all of us. In the construction of race, we all have been assigned a social rank and role in the hierarchical caste system. Within these social rankings and roles, we have *all* been dehumanized. Therefore, we all need to detox and deconstruct from the social and economic stronghold racism has on our lives. We all need to become antiracist. Antiracism is the practice of identifying and opposing racism. We can all learn to do that well. Perhaps because you have been exposed only to Black leaders in the movement, you assume that antiracism centers Black people.

First, don't assume that a Black antiracist is concerned only with Black liberation. We understand that none of us are free until we all are free, as Maya Angelou shared. Antiracism centers justice and belonging for all.

Second, don't feel excluded by the so-called Black–White binary. Originally, during the founding of the United States, race was constructed into two-ish categories: enslaved Africans subsequently designated "Black" (Negro); and European colonizers and settlers allowed to profit from land ownership designated as "White." So, when structural and systemic racism is explored in historical contexts, its binary foundation remains central to the conversation. However, after the Civil War, immigration policies played a significant role in redefining and expanding the racial caste system to include all non-White Anglo-Saxton Protestants.

Finally, if you have made the choice to opt out of the opportunity to become antiracist and cultivate justice and belonging in your sphere of influence, please do not criticize the people who take on that responsibility. Regardless of your race and ethnicity, choose to support and work in solidarity with those who are making pathways in the movement for collective liberation. Bear some of the load. Many hands make light work.

5. *My children or students are too young for antiracism. Young children don't see skin color. I don't see skin color.*

Often used by someone who is attempting to sound nonracist, race-based "colorblindness" is the idea that you do not *see* skin color or notice differences in race, or if you do, you do not treat people differently based on race. Colorblindness ideology is problematic in that it suppresses public discourse on race and masks discrepancies in decision-making.

Unfortunately, we've witnessed parents and educators emphatically profess colorblindness—that is, until their child or student exacts racial prejudice, shows signs of internalized racism, or experiences racial *othering*. Othering occurs when an individual or group attributes difference as negative to set themselves apart as an *in-group of belonging* from an *out-group of not belonging*. Othering legitimizes the marginalization, exclusion, and sometimes even violent extinction of out-groups (Marti, personal communication, 2020 [Slack]). Because silence and pretending to not notice phenotypic differences seems easier, many adults want to believe that children do not see skin color and are too young for antiracism. However, the colorblind approach inadvertently teaches children that noticing phenotypic differences (or talking about race/ism) is taboo, bad, or shameful. Generally when children ask questions about skin tone or race, adults delineate to abstractions like, "We are all equal," "We treat everyone the same," "We see only people; we don't see skin color." *Color shaming*, or being racially colorblind or *color mute,* does not give adults or children the skills or language to understand race.

A child's curiosity about phenotypic and social differences is not quenched with "we are all equal." Children see differences in skin color and want to talk about these differences—especially with their peers. In *Rubbing Off* (Greater Good Magazine, Parenting & Family, 2008), Allison Briscoe-Smith, director of diversity, equity, and inclusion at the Wright Institute, sheds some light on the developmental process of children:

For years, studies have found that children who recognize these [skin tone or racial] differences from an early age show a stronger general ability to identify subtle differences between categories like color, shape, and size—which, in turn, has been linked to higher performance on intelligence tests. . . . Children between the ages of 4 and 7 who show this advanced ability to identify and categorize differences are actually less prejudiced. So parents, rest assured: When children notice and ask about racial differences, it's a normal and healthy stage of development.

It is natural for children to make distinctions and categorize. But parents and teachers who have ascribed to being racially colorblind have little experience talking about skin tone and race without feeling like they are somehow being racist or contributing to race problems.

Babies notice skin tone differences as early as 6–18 months. By age 3, preschoolers group themselves based on differences like race and sex and make decisions to associate with friends who look like them. By age 5, even when it is not discussed, children see skin tone phenotype—what we call race—as a major point of difference or distinction. By age 7, children can accurately reflect social status bias and will make choices or judgments based on who they perceive as having more power or privilege (Bigler, Averhart, and Liben, 2003). Also, by age 7, White children demonstrate that they believe children of color experience less pain than they do (Dore et al., 2014).

Even when children are told that people are all the same, White kids continue to demonstrate stronger racial biases than children of other groups (We Stories, 2013). Our children and students are simply trying to make sense of our hyper-racialized society where they are being told that everyone is the same. They need an understanding of how race/ism has formed the social context in which they live, learn, and play.

If you shut down their curiosity or don't give children language and permission, you may not have the privilege of observing them talk about phenotypic and social differences. Trust us, when we show up in their learning spaces and give them language and space to ask questions, they talk to us—incessantly! Children have questions. They want answers. Because their brains are meaning-making, storytelling machines, children (and most adults) create narratives to fill in information gaps. For example, a White child may think that because their classmate's skin is brown, it must be dirty. And because a parent or teacher has not taught them the truth, they may then take their inquiry to their brown-skinned classmate. This could result in an injurious exchange between the two children. Let's give children the language to be able to affirm and see the beauty in themselves and others.

6. *This won't cost me anything. I don't need to invest much. I can simply attend a workshop, seminar, conference, or continuing education course about racism.* We love that we get to lead professional development for schools,

districts, and PTA workshops for parents. However, as we mentioned previously, addressing root systems, engaging in heart work, and embodying an intention and commitment to teaching for justice and belonging requires much more than attending a one-time event. Teaching for justice and belonging is a long-term investment. It is easy to engage in a workshop and hear content that aligns with your beliefs and allows you to maintain the status quo. However, when your beliefs or behaviors are challenged, you may experience discomfort. This is the time to stay engaged and lean into what you are learning.

There will be so much you didn't know that you didn't know. The only way to know more is to engage more. This growth process may also cost you peers, friends, or even family. As you begin your growth journey, you may have people around you who don't want you to talk about race or justice. They may begin to exclude you from gatherings and planning meetings. You may be treated unfavorably. Experiencing rejection due to someone's discomfort comes with the territory. You may grow, and they may not.

Along the way, you will gain much, but you may lose some as well. So be prepared.

In our experience, we have observed that the healthiest and most self-sustaining change occurs incrementally over time rather than instantaneously. Oftentimes, we are summoned to help adults recover from a racism-related crisis, like an incident in the community, school, or home. Typically, and understandably, a speedy solution is expected. However, like a Band-Aid, a speedy solution addresses only the wound and not its cause. And while it is important that we act urgently to end the crisis, sustainable efforts begin when we allow ourselves to grow from the crisis.

The Seed Growth Metaphor

We liken a sustainable and enduring growth process to that of a seed. The life cycle of a seed is purposeful, consistent, and persistent. A seed is endowed with growth intelligence. We cannot force a seed to grow and produce fruit. Soil is infused with nutrients to help the seed grow roots, sprout, and press to the earth's surface. Over time with the right conditions, nutrients, and care, what was once a mere seed grows, blooms, and ultimately bears fruit for all to enjoy.

We have noticed that people often want the fruit of a just and belonging community, but they don't understand or want to invest time in the cultivating process. Once, after a day of professional development, a school principal told us that he was only really interested in the second part of the presentation. The first half of the presentation is where we shared history, context, and an analytical lens that undergirds the application and practices that we offered during the second half of the presentation. The principal wanted a little fruit without the understanding, substance, and commitment to sustain a growth process. He wanted tasks to perform.

This school principal's sentiment is not uncommon. He wanted teachers to conclude the professional development session with measurable strategies and action steps. We understand this technical approach. But as we've witnessed, parents, schools, and communities that root themselves in an extended growth process are not easily plucked from the garden and do eventually bear fruit. We know that checking a to-do list is immediately gratifying, but we are encouraging you to commit to an extended growth cycle—one rooted in purpose and that requires consistency and persistence. Because there was no commitment to a sustained growth process, years later that school continues to lack sustainable vision and direction regarding justice and belonging. After only one introductory professional development workshop, they considered themselves proficient. And when their students' parents suggested that the school staff receive additional support for diversity, equity, and belonging training, parents were met with a performative reply: "We already worked with Dr. Glass and Dr. Berry." However, when we had offered development and support beyond the introductory workshop, the school leaders failed to follow through.

Consider this a cautionary tale. We will reap what we sow. We have been working with schools, districts, and universities that have invested years into antiracism, justice, and belonging. And while these schools are not where they want to be, they are at least well on their way. Schools and other learning communities that begin by casting a vision for at least 5 years set the expectation for a committed learning process. They understand how we learn. One workshop cannot offer enough time and content to gain proficiency and competency in any complex subject matter—learning to do your taxes, understanding social media algorithms, growing the garden of your dreams.

As you make your way through *Teaching for Justice and Belonging*, the close of each chapter offers prompts for reflection and practice, which we hope you find useful. At the end of the book, we also offer a curated list of resources that will help you continue to grow your knowledge, understanding, and practice. While you will primarily hear from the two of us, we also share the voices and stories of parents and teachers who want to encourage you in your growth process. Each story shared in first person is marked by the storyteller's name.

Tehia

This journey of justice and belonging began for me as a young student. I am from San Diego, California, which is a very diverse city. All my schools were racially, linguistically, and socioeconomically diverse. I was a Black girl from a low-income household. My intuition told me that some of my elementary teachers didn't like me. Back then, I didn't have the sophisticated language to say that my teachers held negative biases and prejudices toward me because I was Black and from a family with low income. They talked to and treated me differently than some of my peers. It was painful. I also had some great teachers who invested in me despite my being a poor Black girl. That was comforting. My teacher, Ms. D., recommended me for a gifted and talented education (GATE) program. My mom and dad loved the idea, but I immediately noticed that there were not many kids who looked like me in the GATE classes. What I also noticed is that the GATE classes were not fun and felt like extra busy work. There were lots of worksheets and bland activities, but nothing that really engaged my mind. So I begged my parents to pull me out of the GATE. When the school year was over, they complied with my wishes.

I had some of my favorite and best teachers in high school and undergrad. I was a part of the AVID program (Advancement Via Individual Determination), which was a college preparation program for low-income and historically marginalized students. My teachers gave us space to just be and to acknowledge that it is cool to be smart and to question the world. Thank you, Mr. Madigan! After high school, I went to Bethune-Cookman College (BCC), now University, a small, private HBCU. I found my place at BCC. I was validated, affirmed, and saw my reflection in the curriculum, my professors, and the general culture of the institution. Because all of the faculty, staff, and upperclass students told us so, excellence was expected, and it didn't have to look a particular way.

So, when I became a teacher, I prepared my predominately Black second-grade class to be the best students they could be. I tried to affirm the value and importance of their racial identity. To foster high race-esteem, I infused Black history into every aspect of the curriculum so they could see themselves. I didn't have the academic prowess then to know that I was being culturally responsive or liberatory in my teaching; I just wanted them to have what I didn't have in elementary school—mirrors and validation that it was okay to be a smart, Black kid. I wanted them to experience a classroom free of racial bias and know that learning is fun.

My teaching continued into graduate school. I taught under-graduate and graduate students educational technology in my master's program at the University of Northern Iowa, and multicultural education–diversity and cognition and instruction in my educational psychology PhD program at the University of Nebraska. Throughout my graduate studies, race and culture were cornerstones in my teaching, research, service, and dissertation. As I prepared preservice teachers to go into their own classrooms, they needed to be prepared to affirm and validate the diversity of students who awaited them. Some of them didn't appreciate the internal work or introspection. I had them explore their own biases as they completed their field placements in schools with children of color. Some students did not like that and critiqued me in my course evaluations. They complained that diversity had nothing to do with a course on child development. It absolutely does! However, year after year, students return and thank me. They appreciate that I saw them as future teachers and prepared them to acknowledge and challenge their biases. After more than 20 years of teaching, I never get tired of former students returning to say thank you. I invest in them so they can invest in the next generation of children.

After applying for and awarded tenure at my university, I thought it was time to get married and have my own children. I knew how I wanted to parent my boys, but I had no idea it would be so difficult. The world we live in is rough, and it consistently shows me the ways that it devalues Black people. Having Black boys meant that my partner and I were going to have to be intentional and proactive in helping them understand their racial identity and giving them affirming language.

Lucretia

As a child, I excelled in formal education. School is where I felt like I belonged. Perhaps because I am naturally perceptive and analytical, while in elementary school I noted the significant effort dedicated to teaching about White America. This was in stark juxtaposition to the lack of teaching about Black America. Back then, my world was socially segregated into Black and White. I was born into a Black family. We belonged to a Black church. Outside of attending a racially integrated school, I lived a Black life. Fortunately, I learned about and lived a Black American life outside the school's formal instruction.

Though I had great teachers, my parents often took care to amend harmful perspectives taught at school. For example, when my sweet, well-meaning, southern, White history teacher taught that American chattel slavery wasn't "that bad"—that enslavers treated their slaves like family—I ran home to tell my mom the good news. My mother revealed all the holes in that erroneous White-washed version of the story and helped me see why and how my teacher benefited from her telling of history.

Then there was the time when a teacher sang the praises of American meritocracy. She shared that in America if you worked really hard you could be wealthy and become whatever you wanted. Once again, I told my mom the good news, to which she responded, "How can that be true? The slaves worked harder than anyone and got nothing!" My parents were teaching me to think critically and see structural flaws. Meanwhile, my school asked me to swallow and digest a particular narrative that excluded my heritage and humanity.

In a racially integrated school, where justice and belonging were not carefully and mindfully cultivated, there was bound to be overt interpersonal racism. I recall a fellow fifth grader who called us Black students monkeys and announced that he wished we lived back in the time of slavery. The teacher agreed with him. Actually, the teacher said, "Look at how y'all are behaving! I don't blame him!" And then there was my chemistry teacher, who, when I scored a 100 on a test, chuckled as he responded, "I didn't know Black people were that smart." I was shocked and devastated. I expected more from a teacher. I was disappointed that someone entrusted with the responsibility to shape minds would flippantly spout off such a degrading comment. Needless to say, that day I lost respect for that teacher and lost interest in his course.

In middle and high school, I didn't know the terms for it, but I observed *structural racism* and *racial bias* at work. I noticed that peers with whom I had shared classrooms since elementary school were no longer in my classes. We were being sorted and tracked academically into categories like remedial, basic, honors, and advanced. I noticed that White students were tracked upward into advanced and honors courses, while most Black students were in basic and remedial level courses. Because I excelled academically, I was tracked with the White students.

After graduating from high school, I attended South Carolina State University, an HBCU, where belonging was the air I breathed— where being Black and academically gifted was normal, supported, and expected. I was reimmersed into a historically, exclusively White formal learning environment when I completed my graduate degrees at Iowa State University, a HWI. While earning a doctorate in education (with a focus in curriculum and instruction, multicultural education, instructional technology), I had the opportunity to formulate ideas and design instruction that centered justice and belonging.

I feel fortunate to have grown up in a community that afforded me a perspective different from the one handed to me in my early school years. Now, as a wife in an interracial marriage and a mom of three multiethnic daughters, I have intentionally and meticulously centered justice and belonging in our home and family. Doing so has required my husband and me to actively disrupt the racialized norms that marginalize our family and specifically our children. Parents of multiethnic children are challenged with reinforcing a sense of belonging as our families navigate a society that often defines "us and them" along racial lines. We, without hesitation, choose competence over colorblind ideology, courage over fear, and the power of creativity over the impotence of the status quo.

* * *

Together, we are inspired and committed to supporting you—our colaboring parents, educators, and teacher leaders—in normalizing justice as a precedent instead of a punishment. We understand that you want to be a conduit of belonging in justice-centered spaces for every child in your charge. As adults who want to raise healthy children, we have to make sense of our achieved racial and ethnic identities before we can prepare our children for a racialized society that has, historically and contemporarily, had a difficult time formulating helpful dialogue on race. Whether we choose to talk about it or not, we enact and experience race/ism on a daily basis—personally and systemically. Racism influences disparities in income, wealth, education, criminality, and health. We want to help prepare you to raise the generation that will dismantle structural injustice and craft a society that values all. We can give our children what we did not have: a sophisticated schema, or a conceptual system for understanding our social influences.

Growth begins right where you are. We understand that you may fear the unknown, but do not allow fear to stop you from embracing the lessons and liberty that the learning journey offers. Like you, we too had a beginning. And we continue to grow. We are here to help you build your capacity for embodying antiracism without feeling overwhelmed. Our primary goal is to help you understand that deep growth takes time—more time than you may think.

The next section contains your first set of prompts for reflection. Use them to nurture your growth. Be vulnerable. Resist the urge to say or write the socially acceptable answer. Challenge yourself to address your deepest thoughts and feelings. Only then can you begin to grow. Uproot the weeds of shame, performative behavior, and judgment (of yourself and others). When weeds are extracted, there is more space for good seeds to germinate, grow, and flourish. Also, to extend your processing, we have curated a list of resources organized by chapter at the end of the book—more to read, listen to, and watch.

Reflection and Practice
REFLECTION

1. Cultivating justice and belonging requires deep critical reflection and introspection. As educators and parents, we must begin with ourselves—examining personal and social identities, reflecting on our own values, and acknowledging how our biases influence relationships with our students. What are your earliest memories of race? When did you realize that race denotes meaning and plays a significant role in how you see yourself and people?

2. Do you see connections to Tehia or Lucretia? What in their stories resonates with you?

3. Are you ready to embark on a growth journey to create space in your heart, home, and classroom to cultivate justice and belonging? Why or why not?

PRACTICE

1. Write about your own schooling and how race may have impacted your experience—where you lived, where you went to school, what you learned, who your friends were, who your teachers were, who was tracked for college or graduate school and who was not.

2. Create a Know, Want to Know, What you Learned, How You Learned It Chart (see Appendix A). As you prepare yourself for this journey, notate what you know, and what you want to know. List those items. Then, at the end of the book, list what you learned, and how you learned it.

3. In this chapter, we listed some common misunderstandings and missteps that might distance you from a transformative antiracism journey. Highlight or list the ones that are significant to you. List other obstacles that have kept you from getting a good start.

CHAPTER 2
SOIL: The Groundwork

When a flower doesn't bloom, you fix the environment in which it grows, not the flower.

—Alexander Den Heijer, Inspirational Speaker

In our garden, laying the groundwork allows us to provide the right conditions for growth. Healthy, sustainable gardens need healthy soil. Soil houses the root structure for upright growth; provides seeds and plants with essential nutrients, minerals, and air; and protects against destructive activity. For the purpose of our metaphorical garden, soil is likened to our foundation. To yield the right fruit, we must take account of our soil—the environment in which we will grow. We must take account of ourselves, our children, other parents, teachers, teacher leaders, our neighborhood, and our historical, cultural, and social norms. We must also examine our hearts. Can healthy seeds be nurtured in our hearts? Is our community compatible or ready for the growth we want? Do we understand what growth requires?

* * *

On the first day of school, Lucia, an African American sixth grader, was bullied by a group of White boys on the bus ride home. They asked Lucia if she was Black. She said yes. In fact, she was the only Black student on the bus. The White boys proceeded to tell racist jokes about Black people to entertain themselves and other White students.

"What do you call a group of Black people?" the boy asked.

"A slave auction!" he shouted.

When Lucia arrived home and told her parents, they immediately dropped what they were doing and headed to the school. The school director was appalled. He suspended the boys for a significant amount of time.

We wish we could write that we extracted Lucia's story from the history of 1957 school desegregation. But White boys deemed it appropriate to entertain themselves at the expense of an African American 11-year-old girl in 2021!

* * *

Before we examine Lucia's story for lessons and growth opportunities, let's make sure we understand common yet significant terms used in antiracism discourse. We heard someone say, "Clarity is kind," and we agree. To create shared solutions, we must have a shared vision and engage in shared problem-solving. Therefore, we must have a common or shared understanding. We have observed that the best intentions can be thwarted when a mutual understanding of common words has not been established. For example, *race*, *nationality*, *culture*, and *ethnicity* denote four completely different social identities, yet they are often used interchangeably. When addressing racism, interchanging *race* with *nationality* and *culture* is problematic in that the former includes a distinctly different historical and social basis from the latter two. Cultivating justice and belonging requires us to understand and address how the ideology of race/ism deprives us of collective community goals.

As we offer understanding—to adults and children—our approach is both relational and pedagogical. We are all connected, so we have to be relational in behavior and pedagogical in our approach. We make no assumptions or judgments about where people should be. Our fundamental philosophy or belief is to examine the systems that have prohibited people from reaching their goals and aspirations. Years ago, we heard John A. Powell, leader of University of California–Berkeley's Othering & Belonging Institute, remind us to be "hard on systems and soft on people." The many systems with which we interact (e.g., education, housing, health care, employment, criminal, legal) have formed us, our communities, and our lifestyles. When we can address how the systems have contributed to and shaped injustice and exclusion, we can support people who want to dismantle and disrupt such systems.

Much of the disconnect between the problem and progression to the solution is due to our lack of shared language. Irish playwright and political activist George Bernard Shaw is credited with pointing out that "Britain and America are two nations divided by a common language." He makes the point that even though we use the same words, due to cultural differences, those words often have distinctly different meanings. Likewise, common words like race, racism, and justice are used in mainstream dialogue but have distinctly different, often more nuanced and specific meanings in fields of study that help us understand the impact of systems like sociology, psychology, and law. Shared language helps us forge connections. Let's begin with a mutual understanding and clarity regarding common but significant terms.

Tehia

Do you remember learning how to read? I don't. I just remember reading. However, someone taught me. When I ask my antiracism graduate certificate students how they arrived at their meanings of *race, racism*, and *antiracism*, they can't remember where they got them; they just have them. My students were blown away by how differently words commonly associated with race were defined by research scholars. Our understanding of terms like race and racism varied. If we had not gained a more sophisticated, nuanced, academically informed understanding of such common terms, we would not have been able to hold a cohesive or helpful conversation. With a mutual understanding, we were able to learn from one another.

In fall 2020, I organized my History and Psychology of Racism syllabus to discuss voting rights and political events in conjunction with Election Day. I wanted my students to see the way politicians use race/ism. They were able to see a type of racially coded manipulation unfold in real time and in real life. They learned about what Ian Haney Lopez describes as "dog whistles" in his 2013 book *Dog Whistle Politics—How Coded Racial Appeals Have Reinvented Racism and Wrecked the Middle Class.* I received the following email (Figure A.1) after one of the presidential debates:

> Good Morning Dr. Glass,
>
> I was watching the debate last night and when Biden referenced dog whistle politics, I jumped from my seat because I knew what that meant based on our materials this week. Well done! I consider myself to be lucky to be in this program and I appreciate what you all are doing for us and the nation! I hope you have a great day today!
>
> Sincerely,

My student was able to listen to the debate and witness how coded language is used to covertly appeal to and stoke fear and agency in some people while appearing to be free of racial bias. Because we had conversations about terms and language, he saw the parallels.

* * *

Race

Race has a story and a history. Race was created, manifested, and preserved via beliefs, behaviors, policies, and practices. Race is not biologically real but was and is socially and politically constructed through laws, public policies, and social practices. When we talk about race here, we are not reducing this sophisticated, complicated, and nuanced construct to an acknowledgment of skin tone differences. Race entails a massive constitution that impacts almost every aspect of our modern lives.

To help you understand race, we offer this explanation informed by Dr. Gerardo Marti, William R. Kenan, Jr. Professor of Sociology at Davidson College. Race categorizes people based on the presumption of shared physical and biological characteristics. As White Europeans colonized and enslaved groups, racial categories became a crucial means of sustaining their dominant relations of power and privilege.

Over time, the racial hierarchy became institutionalized. For example, a fair-brown-skinned, multiethnic person could be racially categorized in the United States as Black, in South Africa as Colored, and in Brazil as White. The public policies and social practices of these countries established their own distinct racial categories in conjunction with sustaining power dynamics.

Marti contends that among the personal consequences of such categories is that identities are forced to "fit" into racial categories on the assumption that they reflect a person's ancestral heritage. The most important societal consequence is the legitimation of gaps in equality of wealth, opportunity, and access to other valuable resources like education. He adds:

> An additional complication in the United States is that racial policies could differ dramatically by state, most obviously in the distinction between slave and free states. Local governments most often administered benefits, funding programs, and voting privileges—such that the racial divide between White settler colonialists and the indigenous and people of color were subject to a variety of changing standards and expectations over the majority of our American history. (personal communication, November 4, 2021 [Slack])

Racial distinctions are highly problematic in that they convey a concreteness that has been repeatedly shown to lack biological validity, However, these distinctions become real through their ongoing social enactment—personally, organizationally, and societally—in every arena of our social world, including day-to-day *microaggressions*, pervasive stigmas, exclusionary policies, and lack of adequate laws.

Racism

Contrary to popular misunderstanding, racism is not just individual racial prejudice, hatred, or discrimination. Instead, racism is an oppressive force that creates and reproduces a complex system of social inequality. It involves one group having the power to carry out systematic discrimination through the major institutions of society, which is a byproduct of racial categorization that focuses on the hierarchical arrangement of various racial groups.

Essentially, racism is a combination of social and institutional power, race prejudice, White supremacy, and oppression that thrives through systems and individuals. Systemic racism is perpetuated through social institutions like schools and courts of law and structurally through public policies and institutional practices. As individuals, we sustain racism when we internalize racist messaging and succumb to racist beliefs and practices. For example, the Fair Housing Act of 1968 sought to end the Federal Housing Administration's (FHA) discriminatory practices that kept Black Americans in neighborhoods with fewer education and job opportunities than White neighborhoods, essentially creating a geography of race. However, real estate agents continued to exacerbate the normalcy of race-based spaces by preventing buyers from entering certain neighborhoods—not showing Black buyers homes in predominantly White neighborhoods and vice versa.

White Space

Most explicitly in its formative history, White institutions have often been established with the expectation that people of color would be excluded. Indeed, history shows that all major institutions in the United States are found to have been established as White spaces— the U.S. Constitution, representation in Congress, citizenship, state government, courts, public schools, religious institutions, colleges, and the list goes on. Therefore, White spaces are social situations and organizational practices designed by White people for themselves to advance their own collective interests and to maintain domination. Following the Civil War, and more specifically after the 1964 Civil Rights Act, some White spaces began to open to people of color. However, their foundation remained rooted in Whiteness.

Because they relieve the psychological burden of uncomfortably invoking or reproducing exclusionary practices against people of color, White spaces require no overt enforcement. When White spaces are naturalized for White people, they legitimize the enjoyment of exclusionary spaces and allow inhabitants to remain racially ignorant about racism. Within White spaces, racial ignorance is inevitable and racism is delegated to organizational apparatuses—rules, traditions, cultural norms, a good fit—that obscure the broader racial domination in which white spaces are rooted.

Whiteness
Whiteness is not inherently determined but is defined socially and legally by a commonsense understanding of being a member of the White race, which serves to elevate people who are racialized as White over people who are not. Whiteness identified as the normal and centric racial identity grants access to opportunities and privileges not available to other groups.

Racial Ignorance
Jennifer C. Mueller, associate professor of sociology at Skidmore College, describes racial ignorance as the presence of false or mystified beliefs and the absence of understandings, feelings, and moral judgments regarding racial structures. Racial ignorance is a cognitive accomplishment grounded in practices of knowing and not-knowing that result in misinterpretations of racism—historic and current. Subsequently, racial ignorance allows various forms of racial injustice and racial oppression to be seen as normal or natural and therefore should not be challenged or contested. For example, claiming colorblindness is a mechanism of racial ignorance, which suppresses understanding to avoid discomfort, social tensions, or a reliving of personal trauma. As with colorblindness, racial ignorance requires a rational commitment and ongoing effort to disregard race, racism, and racial domination.

Microaggression
Directed at a culturally, racially, or ethnically marginalized group, microaggressions are subtle but offensive comments or actions that often unintentionally or unconsciously reinforce a stereotype. For example, a White person may express an intended compliment to a Black person by saying, "I don't see you as Black." The racist premise is that Black is bad, unattractive, unintelligent, or less than human.

Microaggressors are often not aware that they are reinforcing a frame and narrative of *racism*.

Justice

Often when people hear the word *justice*, they think retribution. We found a more accurate and helpful description through The Bible Project in which justice is described as restorative. In their 2017 YouTube video, Justice, The Bible Project portrays justice as a radical, selfless way of life that involves seeking out, advocating for, and helping vulnerable people and changing social structures to prevent injustice. They maintain that justice means nurturing right relationships between people and treating others as the image of God.

In *The Little Book of Race and Restorative Justice*, Fania Davis (2019) describes justice as individual and collective growth and healing. She discusses the collectivist versus individual mindset, where we take care of one another and are accountable to self and others. We acknowledge that our collective freedom is tied to one another.

Ernest Boyer's (1990) six principles of community describe a just learning environment as one where the sacredness of each person is honored and where diversity is aggressively pursued. What does this look like in practice? A just learning space is one that educationally, not just socially, builds a shared racial, ethnic, and cultural understanding. So that social relationships can be put in context, formal instruction is dedicated to teaching and learning about the heritage, traditions, perspectives, histories, and lived experiences of ethnic groups beyond those who are racialized as White. A just learning community intentionally cultivates respect and value for differences while simultaneously defining the shared values of the learning community members.

Teaching for justice requires us to actively overcome barriers so that every child has the opportunity to be seen, safe, valued, and inspired. To do this, we get to challenge racial, social, cultural, and economic injustices imposed on students resulting from a differential distribution of opportunities and resources. Not only must we be dedicated to implementing change and reform in schools, but we must also be clear about manifesting educational equity.

Belonging

Our favorite working definition of belonging is described by Radha Agrawal in her 2018 book *Belong*:

> It's a feeling of home, of "I can exhale here and be fully myself with no judgment or insecurity." Belonging is about shared values and responsibility, and the desire to participate in making your community better. It's about pride, showing up, and offering your unique gift to others. *You can't belong if you only take.* (p. 17)

Belonging warrants support and a sense of identity, acceptance, security, and inclusion. Peering through a belonging lens, we are prompted to question whether we or our children and students can thrive in our current learning spaces. Are we bringing our authentic selves, and can they bring their authentic selves and feel at home in our homes, classrooms, schools?

Belonging and inclusion are not synonymous. Inclusion extends an invitation to those historically excluded to participate in existing social structures without fundamental change to those structures. However, to cultivate belonging, we are required to identify and challenge structures established and sustained by excluding lives, experiences, and stories. For example, practicing inclusion allows a system of education designed primarily for White students to now invite previously excluded students to the learning space. Meanwhile, belonging anchors a narrative that weaves together multiple perspectives and values a participatory vision. Therefore, a system of education previously designed to marginalize students who are not White must be reconsidered and redesigned.

When we cultivate a garden of belonging, new plantings or opportunities sprout for designing and creating an alternative structure. Such belonging builds our capacity to:

- ◆ Fortify our connections to each other and place
- ◆ Ensure that we thrive and not simply survive
- ◆ Distribute power equitably
- ◆ Value the dignity of every student or child

Antiracism

Though practicing antiracism requires a commitment to a difficult course of action, its definition is simple. Antiracism is the policy or practice of identifying and actively opposing racism. Essentially, antiracism is the antithesis to racism. It is the antivenom to racism's envenomation. Alex Zamalin (2019) describes antiracism as "historical consciousness and attentiveness to social structure and political choices informed by power" (p. 127). Zamalin moves beyond the idea of bad actors of racism and identifies systems that contribute to anti-Black racism, which he considers the most "expansive, historically durable, and salient form [of racism] in America" (p. 7). He emphasizes that historically, people have organized to defeat the social structures that oppress via power.

Antiracism is a lifelong process of actively identifying and opposing racial prejudice and systemic racism. Structured around conscious efforts and deliberate actions, antiracism cultivates equitable opportunities for all people on an individual and a systemic level. Because it requires us to actively dismantle structures, systems, and practices that produce social injustices, antiracism is essential to cultivating justice and belonging.

* * *

To position ourselves to promote justice and belonging, we acknowledge personal privilege (e.g., education, social economic status, opportunities for social mobility, social capital); acknowledge and work to change personal racial biases; and confront and disrupt acts and systems of racial discrimination. We engage in a consistent cycle of unlearning and learning. This growth cycle entails constant observation and reflection. We encourage you to consistently ask yourself the following questions:

- What was I taught?
- How does what I was taught differ from what I am now learning, reading, and experiencing in this context?
- How do I reconcile the difference?

- For example, how are the operational definitions of *race, racism, justice, belonging,* and *antiracism* different from what you may have been taught?
- What does it look like to come to terms with the difference?

We also want you to get good at examining and challenging structures and systems that have shaped unjust and exclusionary practices. Dr. Jewell Cooper, professor and associate dean for academic affairs and student services in the School of Education at University of North Carolina–Greensboro, offers a practical framework for analyzing public discourse, decision-making, and policies (2014). She reminds us that with every decision made, someone is advantaged, and someone may be disadvantaged. As teachers, parents, and leaders of education, we must consistently ask ourselves:

- Who is marginalized or reduced to a position of minimal importance, influence, or power by this policy, rule, statement, belief, or instruction?
- Who benefits?
- Who made the policy or rule?
- Who created the standard?
- Who is impacted?
- How are people with social advantages seen, valued, and encouraged?
- How are people who have been marginalized seen, valued, and encouraged?

Normalizing this practice of reflection and analysis helps us to be mindful of our environment—the history and context in which we are working. Also, asking these questions allows us to see and acknowledge structures and policies that impact our lives but seem invisible or inconspicuous. American physician, epidemiologist, and antiracism activist Dr. Camara Phyllis Jones (2000) uses a gardening allegory to illustrate how, as gardeners—parents, teachers, teacher leaders—we must know our environment. In *Levels of Racism*, Jones shares:

> When my husband and I bought a house in Baltimore, there were 2 large flower boxes on the front porch. When spring came we decided to grow flowers in them. One of the boxes was empty, so we bought potting soil to fill it. We did nothing to the soil in the other box, assuming that it was fine. Then we planted seeds from a single seed packet in the 2 boxes. The seeds that were sown in the new potting soil quickly sprang up and flourished. All of the seeds sprouted, the most vital towering strong and tall, and even the weak seeds made it to a middling height. However, the seeds planted in the old soil did not fare so well. Far fewer seeds sprouted, with the strong among them only making it to a middling height, while the weak among them died. It turns out that the old soil was poor and rocky, in contrast to the new potting soil, which was rich and fertile. The difference in yield and appearance in the 2 flower boxes was a vivid, real-life illustration of the importance of environment. (p. 1213)

Clearly, the soil impacted the seed's growth. But often we fail to investigate and question systems or the larger culture at work—that is, the soil. Finally, this reflective practice helps you grow your capacity to problem-solve. You can't heal what is not revealed. When you examine structures, systems, rules, and policies, you begin to see a whole person within the problem instead of a "broken person" as the problem.

Now that you have definitions for common but often misunderstood terms and a framework for discerning and examining policies that shape practices and behavior, you can assess your environment and begin to lay the groundwork for growth. Consider how people racialized as White historically designed White spaces to exclude people of color. Are you in a historically White space? Contemplate how racial ignorance, which frames racial injustice as normal and natural and allows us to avoid discomfort, requires us to abdicate our power and responsibility to create justice and belonging for all students and children. Meanwhile, an antiracism practice, liberatory and fundamental to our foundation, is often weaponized and framed as dangerous.

Within Lucia's story, think about the roles that race, racism, Whiteness, White space, and racial ignorance played in manifesting her experience. The White boys were suspended for their overt interpersonal racism. You might think that a lengthy suspension means that justice prevailed. But ask yourself, did the act of suspending the boys make Lucia feel safe? How will she feel when the boys return to school and the bus? Will she ever feel safe and valued at school? Will school be a space where she can exhale and fully be herself with no judgment or insecurity about her racial identity or how her peers see her? Will she ever feel as though she belongs? Though her bullies were suspended, what will it take to expel the trauma from her body? As evident by our stories (Chapter 1), this incident may become a formidable chapter in Lucia's life story. And finally, who will help the boys reconcile their behavior and grow from this experience?

Reflection and Practice

REFLECTION

1. How does reading about Lucia's traumatizing incident make you feel?
2. What would you do if Lucia was your daughter or student? How would you help her recover and heal?
3. What definitions are different from what you anticipated?
4. Identify policies or rules (historic and current) that have helped shape the social demographic of your neighborhood and school.

PRACTICE

1. If you have not already, participate in an educational course or program to help you understand (1) how misconceptions surrounding the concept of race are shaped by our history, social institutions, and cultural beliefs, and (2) the role that racist policies and practices played in shaping our communities (neighborhood, school, church, demographics). If you need help, at the end of the book, we offer suggested resources organized by chapter.

2. As parents, teachers, and teacher leaders, we must become racially aware so that we can reckon with racial injustice. Write a narrative that explores how race has manifested in your life. Creating a racial autobiography is an empowering beginning to your journey. Locating yourself in the context of our country's racial history secures your "why." Identify key realizations, events, and moments across your life and write your personal story around race. Gooden (2021) recommends that you look for points where race came up and explore how you addressed it. If you did not address it, why not? Organize these points along a spectrum, from your earliest learning experiences all the way to the present. We have listed a few questions to guide you.

- Do you think of yourself as a member of a racial or ethnic group? What is its importance to you?
- What was the racial demographic of the neighborhood where you grew up?
- What was your first awareness of race—that there are different "races" and that you are a member of a racial group?
- What were your cultural influences, for example, media, advertisements, fairy tales, music, anecdotes? What phenotypic images of God, angels, Santa Claus, the tooth fairy, or others were shared with you?
- What did you learn about your racial self?
- What did you learn about racial others?
- Who taught you?
- What were the normative behaviors in your home that you considered the default?
- When did you realize there were other ways of thinking and doing things?
- During your high school years, what was America's or your community's racial social climate?
- What is the racial demographic of where you live and work currently? Of your friends? Are your needs met?
- Regarding race, what encounter, moment, or events stand out to you? Did you feel privileged or threatened?

CHAPTER 3
SEED: Self-Assessment

A seed neither fears light nor darkness, but uses both to grow.
—Matshona Dhliwayo, Philosopher, Entrepreneur, Author

Contained in a seed is the potential for growth, beauty, and fruit—essentially, new life. In the right conditions, a seed can grow into a whole new plant. It can replicate itself over successive seasons and years, disperse, and thrive for some time. Inherent in a seed is the substance and possibility to support the early stages of growth and development in a plant. A seed can nourish the embryo, remain dormant during unfavorable conditions, and expand to liberate the root and shoot, which ultimately becomes a bud.

* * *

"What do I do?"
"What do I do next?"
We hear these questions a lot. The sentiment is genuine, but we believe the better question is *"Where should I begin?"* We understand the desire to show growth and fruit immediately. Parents want their children to appreciate and embrace people whose background is different from their own. Educators want their classrooms and lessons to reflect an appreciation and respect for the stories, identities, perspectives, experiences, interests, and contributions of peoples

who historically have been marginalized. Schools want to center on justice and create spaces of belonging where staff and students from diverse backgrounds feel connected by a common care for humanity. These are grand aspirations and admirable visions. However, it is when such aspirations are first realized within us that we can then manifest them in our families, classrooms, and schools. In this chapter, consider yourself a seed, and let's explore how we learn and then grow.

How We Learn
Tehia

Teachers need to understand how children grow and develop so that we can match the content and curriculum to how students learn. I earned my PhD in educational psychology with a focus on cognition and instruction. I love to explore how children learn and how teachers teach. I am fascinated by the organizational structure of our brain and memory. The human brain can process 11 million bits of information every second. Our brain organizes and stores as much of the incoming information as possible. Many of our experiences are stored in our brains in schemas, or as I like to illustrate to my students, *filing cabinets*. Schemata help us to organize and interpret information (Hammond, 2015) and can drive behaviors and thoughts to become automatic (Ormrod, 2013).

Within our filing cabinets are drawers, and within each drawer are folders. The folders are the experiences we have: what we learn about in school and interactions with others. In each folder are pages with bits of information on them. Those bits of information are the details we store, both consciously and subconsciously. For example, when my son was 1, he developed a schema for a dog. He knew a dog walked on four legs, had a tail, had fur, and barked. When he then saw a cat—another four-legged, furry animal with a tail—my son associated the cat with the dog and barked at the cat. We then had to help him understand the difference between the two.

Sometimes we are aware of what we've learned, but sometimes we aren't. The conscious (aware) and unconscious (unaware) knowledge we acquire becomes our schemata. Hammond (2015) relays that our schema development is also connected to our racial and cultural experiences. Such experiences impact how we teach and learn. For example, we can learn and internalize a stereotype without being overtly taught. A White mom asked, "I have never had a negative experience with an African American man, so why as I am sitting in my car do I lock the car door when he passes by?" Without her permission or recognition, harmful messaging had shaped her schema for interacting with African American men.

The brain stores our experiences and then reconnects with those thoughts and behaviors to strengthen our schema. However, when we encounter something—a person, event, new information—that contradicts our schema, we experience cognitive dissonance. Cognitive dissonance is the feeling of confusion or disequilibrium that results from attempting to hold conflicting beliefs, values, or attitudes. Our brain has to work to understand what is going on.

Years ago, I brought my family with me to a professional conference. My partner travels for work as well and has all the platinum-titanium-plutonium status levels and regularly gets upgrades on flights and hotels. On this trip, our family was upgraded to the concierge (top) level of the hotel. We entered the elevator and pushed the button for the floor of our room. Then a White man entered. He pushed the button for his floor, which was below ours. When we all arrived at his floor first, he stood there assuming that we were getting off on his floor. I let him know that we still had one more floor to go. He responded, "How are y'all on a floor higher than me?" With a confused look on his face, he walked out of the elevator. Before I could respond, the elevator doors closed.

In that White man's mind, my Black family could not be on a higher floor. With a schema informed by White superiority, he thought he was better than us. His cognitive dissonance was expressed through his question and ugly tone as he walked off the elevator. In that 3-second moment, I was in shock. My brain couldn't process the question I was asking myself: Did he just say that? Is this dude for real? I wanted to stop the elevator doors from closing and have a quick conversation with him! His seeds of deficit beliefs caused him to say what he was thinking based on what was in his schema.

Now, if you want to debate or defend this man's thought process as you are reading, I need you to pause, take a deep breath, and ask yourself why. Why do you want to defend his position? The "not all" commentary is neither useful nor productive. Individuals don't just keep racism, bias, and prejudice contained in their bodies, beliefs, and words; they express it through norms and institute it through systems.

Let's imagine past the individual and examine this man's environment—home, church, schooling, for example. His environment helped develop his schema for racial rank. Clearly, in his environment, White people are at the top of the social hierarchy (or *exclusive hotel resort*), and Black people are somewhere, anywhere beneath. Furthermore, what if that man worked, lived, or engaged with Black people on a regular basis? What types of microaggressions or macro White supremacy behavior have they been subjected to?

The beauty of our brains is that they are "malleable organs that respond to the environments we are placed in and the challenges we face" (Eberhardt, 2020, p. 15). Our brains are like a muscle in that we can make them stronger. We can rewire the brain by having more and more diverse experiences to override schemata informed by harmful stereotypes. We can also become aware of our biases that are dangerous to other people.

COGNITIVE LOAD

We want to warn those of you go-getters who want to read this whole book and do all the reflections and practices in a day, or even a week. Our brains and hearts are not microwavable. They need time to process and internalize what we read, learn, and feel. If you try to consume too much of this book too quickly, you will tend toward superficial growth. Neither you nor our children deserve superficial growth.

Processing and trying to retain too much too soon via text and video can contribute to cognitive load, which is when we are taxing our brain to learn and act (with and without media support) at the same time. Cognitive load is the amount of memory being used when learning new information. It's like the memory on your phone or computer—when the usage is high, learning becomes less efficient, or harder to store. To continue with the filing cabinet metaphor, when the drawers or folders have a lot of information coming in at the same time, it is more difficult to store the information efficiently.

Based on Mayer and Moreno's (1998) cognitive load theory (which focuses on multimedia experiences, but I believe is applicable here because our learning is in multimedia formats), there are three types of cognitive load: intrinsic, germane, and extraneous. Intrinsic load is the degree of processing that has to be done with the subject matter that is difficult, or new. For example, there is a lot more intrinsic load for me when I am learning a new statistical method versus when I am learning about new historical information to use in my class. The intrinsic load is high when I am learning statistics; because it is complex to me, I have to be in an environment with no distractions. To make it less overwhelming, I have to use strategies to make sure the information makes it into my schemata, like chunking the information together so I'm not learning the information bit by bit. When I'm learning history, I can chunk the information chapter by chapter because I have other information to connect the new information to. To ensure the information sticks, I often ask myself, What do I recall in that chapter? What was the most important information from that chapter?

The second type of cognitive load is germane load. This is when new information is integrated into existing schemata. When germane load is high, we have more schemata available to integrate the new information. If germane load is low, the brain has to build more schemata for the new information, which makes the intrinsic load high. When germane load is high, it is easier to integrate new information into the schemata that already exist. To efficiently maximize germane load, we want to spend time reflecting on what we learned, think about how old and new information are related, and practice what we've learned. We need opportunities to practice.

Extraneous load is the third type of cognitive load. It actually doesn't have anything to do with learning at all. It is about the *extra* things running in the background of your brain. Examples of extraneous load for me would be my to-do lists: *Did I pay for my boys' extracurricular activities? When is their well visit checkup? What groceries do I need to pick up for my partner to make dinner tonight? Did I respond to that email?* Or maybe I'm playing and replaying a conversation I had with someone: *Ugh, I should've said this instead of that; I need to follow up with them to make sure they got what they needed.* When all those noisy thoughts are running in the background, it's difficult to learn and retain new information. It is difficult for information to be absorbed into schemata when I'm thinking about a hundred other things.

Here is a scenario ripped from the pages (or schema) of antiracism education and training. Often, when people are attending a group session where they should be laser focused on learning, an internal monologue is crowding their hearts and minds:

- *I don't want to say the wrong thing.*
- *I don't want them to think I'm racist.*
- *Did I just commit a microaggression?*
- *Why don't I already know this?*

As you can imagine or perhaps relate, the internal monologue gets in the way of learning. So although we've moved on to something else, the learner is still stuck on a previous point that was made. Because the participant allowed the extraneous load to lead, they missed information that was beneficial for them. Ways we can reduce the extraneous load include centering yourself before you begin a task. So you're not trying to remember all the things you need to do, write down your to-do list. Do a couple of breathing exercises or journal for a few minutes so you can release your thoughts onto paper.

Because of what we know about cognitive load, your brain needs time to process, store, and make new connections to all the new information, thoughts, and experiences. We encourage you to not skip over the reflective and practice activities at the end of each chapter. Let's work with our brains, rather than have our brains work against us. Just like you cannot will a seed to grow quickly, you cannot will yourself to process this content quickly.

Our brains are one of the many tools we have to confront racism. Our hearts, our experiences, and our desire for human connections are also tools to overcome racism. Once our brain becomes critically aware of what we are internalizing, we can decide what goes in the schema. Adults and children can do this. Children are being socialized about who they are on a daily basis. Socialization happens in homes, schools, and the community. From what they watch on television to their phone apps and social media, they are being informed on who is pretty, smart, kind, or fair. Consequently, they are also being socialized on who is ugly, unintelligent, scary, or dangerous. Their brains are making meaning with all of the social messaging. I shared in my TED talk (Starker Glass, 2022) that as caregivers we must tell our children who they are before the world tries to tell them who they are not. We have all had that moment where we realized that we were a particular race. Some of those experiences were good, and some of them were not so good. But we all had them. My line of thought is, if I can tell my boys who they are before the world does, then that first encounter with interpersonal racism may hurt a little less. I know it will happen, but I want it to less painful. If I can help all children see the humanity in one another, maybe there may not be any hurt at all.

Because I grew up in San Diego, California, my school and community environment was very diverse. Black, White, Filipino, Samoan, Mexican, and every combination in between was a representation of my friends and my schooling experiences. As a child and through high school, I *loved* to roller-skate. That was my time to enjoy the latest music, hang out with my friends, and skate. Lacing up my skates allowed me to just be who I was and leave the worries of the world behind. From skating lessons to teen night and all-night skates, I loved being at the skating rink. The rink was also where I had my first racialized experience. I was in sixth grade. I knew I was Black before that, but I don't think I was aware that other people knew I was Black or that Black people had to be Black in a certain way. I was taking a rest at the water fountain, and a Black girl and her friends came up to me and said, "Are you Black or White?" I remember looking at her, confused for a moment, thinking, "I know they see my brown skin. Why would she ask me that?" And after a moment, I responded with, "I'm Black." She gave me the side eye, which indicated that she wasn't convinced. She said, "You're not Black." Then she and her friends skated off as if to dismiss me. I began to wonder if being Black was a good thing or a bad thing. I remember experiencing a moment of cognitive dissonance. The schema I had for myself was being questioned. I looked around the rink, and I realized that though the majority of my friends were from diverse backgrounds, they were not Black. I suppose that because she did not see my Black friends, who were not at the rink that evening, she discounted my racial identity.

That experience stuck with me. I share that experience with my college students when we discuss our first racialized experiences. We all have had that moment when we had to acknowledge race—ours or theirs—and the personal and social implications of this awareness. What did you think of yourself or others racially? Was their race a positive or negative thing? How did you treat yourself or someone else because of race? Furthermore, what was your moment?

When we understand how our brains function—how we consciously and unconsciously store information and how we can do that efficiently through cognitive load—we can reflect on what is already in our schemata and treat ourselves and others accordingly. Then we can engage in a diversity of experiences to help us grow.

How We Grow
LUCRETIA

Before I began my racial healing journey, I was complicit with the misunderstanding that racism touched only Black people. Therefore, my version of cultivating justice and belonging was entirely ethnocentric. I cared only about the liberation, healing, and well-being of African Americans. But during my graduate studies at Iowa State University in 1997, I was introduced to antiracism and multicultural education underscored by a study abroad in post-apartheid South Africa. I began to grow in my understanding of how race was codified, not by biology but by unjust laws and social practices. I grew to realize how racial inequity was established, not by personal choices but by racially coded social mechanisms compounded over time. Once I understood the disease of racism, I understood how it harmed everyone, not just Black people. Because education launched me on my journey, I am adamant in my conviction that much can be gained through formal instruction and good pedagogy rooted in antiracism.

At the same time, the small historically Black campus ministry of which I was a part initiated a shift to become a multiracial church. In other words, we would no longer be a Black church but would actively expand beyond our cultural norms to cultivate a belonging space that includes people who are not Black. Decades before I arrived on the Ames, Iowa, campus, this church was birthed out of the university's Black Cultural Center, which served as a haven for African American cultural identity in the historically White space, amid corn fields. The Black Cultural Center Church had since become home to Black students from all over the country with a shared Christian identity, values, and a desire to be in community with one another.

Historically, to avoid addressing the hypocrisy of racial injustice in a nation touting that all men are created equal, White Christians segregated churches. White Christian enslavers who baptized Africans into a compromised, demented version of Christianity continued to hold their African Christian brothers and sisters in bondage and forced them to worship separately. Subsequently, Black churches matured into their own Christian identity and grew to become a refuge for Black spiritual expression and ground zero for organizing the Civil Rights Movement. In fact, the Montgomery Improvement Association, formed by Ralph D. Abernathy, Edgar Daniel Nixon, Ray Robinson, Dr. Martin Luther King, Jr., and others, organized the movement through a multitude of Black churches and associations. The reliance on nonviolence was both spiritual and strategic. It resonated with the traditions of Black churches. Meanwhile, White churches continued to splinter into more denominations over the conflict between those who wanted to preserve a White supremacy–centered existence and those who wanted to become a just and belonging faith community.

Within this historical context, the notion of worshiping with White Christians felt unsafe to me. I did not want to worship with White people. Meeting academic requirements for courses like multicultural and antiracism education was simple. More challenging and complex was the heart work and mental labor required to transform a refuge established for a Black community into a belonging space where people from various racial groups felt at home. Nurturing such a shift demanded community investment into vision casting, strategic planning, and facilitating personal growth. For example, because music and worship style are significant to any church's culture, we had to be willing to listen to, incorporate, and embody music genres that were outside of our cultural preferences. At that time, I had little to no exposure to Christian music beyond the Black gospel expression, and this adjustment was excruciating.

Collectively, we stepped back from what was normal to us so we could see the culture of our community. We analyzed ways our practices unintentionally barred access to our community. We consulted with people from White churches and with people whose church culture was different from ours. We learned what would make our church more accessible and welcoming to people who are not accustomed to or familiar with Black church culture. We then began to integrate changes that fostered a shift; some changes were abrupt, and some were gradual.

One of the most significant changes made was to the name of the church. The name Black Cultural Center (BCC) church reflected its origins and birthplace. As you can imagine, resolving to remove the historical significance of the name was difficult. But we wanted the new name to reflect a different vision of belonging—Body of Christ Church (BCC). We also made changes at the leadership level. Some Black leaders stepped down from their positions so that White people could be added to the leadership team. In a short time, the White leaders who helped in the planning phase served as liaisons for inviting White people to the church. I know that Black leaders making room for White leaders feels counterintuitive to antiracism. But remember, the goal was to deconstruct the structure that historical racism informed and current practices maintained. White people needed to have the opportunity to be in community with BIPOC in non-White spaces—not as saviors but as servants.

We made cultural adjustments as well. Most of us from Black church backgrounds were accustomed to church services lasting 2–3 hours. But we were told that White people may not be willing to *church* for that length of time. I thought to myself, *Oh well, they can just leave early!* Fortunately, though, I was not the leader. We shortened the length of our church service to about 1.5 hours. Not to worry—the socializing and bonding that had occurred during our lengthier gatherings shifted to an after-church group lunch. These gatherings became fixed, fostered belonging, and helped to cultivate authentic friendships.

To include music and songs beyond the Black gospel music tradition, we chose to integrate additional styles of Christian music into our personal lives. At that time you could purchase cassettes and CDs only by going into a music store. Our pastor encouraged us to "walk to a section of the store that you don't usually visit, and buy from a genre that you don't usually listen to." He encouraged us to cross over the aisle between Black Gospel and White Christian music. We did. New White parishioners integrated Black gospel music into their personal lives, while we Black parishioners infused contemporary White gospel music into ours.

A church, like all institutions, is made up of people from various backgrounds. And with a diversity of lived experiences, each of us engaged in our own personal transformation. Each of us had to be willing to grow within. To contribute to a space that became home to people from various backgrounds, we each had to hold and nurture the vision within ourselves—the way a seed holds the vision for what it will become. Personally, I grew to see White folks as able to become colaborers in dismantling racist ideas and structures instead of only as architects and perpetrators of oppression. I gradually felt more comfortable with White people in an intimate, sacred space, like church. And in this new belonging space, I saw some White parishioners become aware of their own racialized identity and take intentional steps toward antiracism.

I was able to help my church community realize its vision only after I made the decision to grow myself. Fortunately, at that time during my graduate program, I was enrolled in a series of antiracism education courses, where I was introduced to an analytical framework for examining race/ism in the United States. Through formal instruction, I was equipped with a historical, political, and social context for understanding how racism was formed and is sustained. During that semester, I built a sound knowledge base and an understanding of harmful ideologies and systemic dynamics. I also elected to participate in other helpful learning experiences like workshops and conferences. I was able to broaden my awareness of my own racial identity and the racial identity of others in relation to our interconnected society. Like a seed, I embodied the vision for the future church and was able to help manifest it.

When we are aware of how institutions and systems have shaped our thinking and behavior, we can take the responsibility to help reshape and reform—first ourselves, then systems and institutions.

So where do you begin? Like we did, you begin with your own growth. First, take the responsibility to learn beyond reading a book or listening to a speaker. Learning involves processing and organizing, writing, higher order thinking, language, attention, and memory, all interacting with your emotions, behavior, social skills, and learning environment. We understand what learning requires for other life essentials like math, science, and reading. But for some reason, we don't engage in a learning process for antiracism, which is equally significant. Be willing to engage in experiences that expose you to facts, histories, stories, perspectives, ideas, and ideologies that may be new to you. Embrace change. Challenge and adjust cultural norms that keep you from expanding. Grow your own capacity to create change.

A common request we hear is, "Please help us change our school, workplace, or church." We've been asked to "fix" the students when a racist incident occurs in school. Some of the funniest requests are when we are asked how to change a racist in-law. We think it's funny that the racist is always an in-law, never a blood relative! Before we can equip our children and students, heal our school community, or help our in-laws, we must begin with ourselves. Beginning with you is the most accessible but most challenging of this growth journey. Zoom in and reflect on your own thinking and practices that could stunt your growth toward a new vision.

Also, zoom out and examine structures and policies that were originally and historically designed to sustain exclusivity—for example, White spaces created by White people to center Whiteness. Learn the history of where you live, teach, and work. Be curious about its roots, how it came to be what it is—racially, ethnically, culturally, and economically. Be willing to challenge anecdotal information and cultural norms that do not align with your new vision. For example, read authors, scholars, activists, and theologians that are outside your cultural bubble—the sociocultural context in which you immerse yourself (Henriques, 2014). Actually, make deliberate efforts to step outside your cultural bubble. One of the best and most reliable ways to do this is to interact with and develop relationships with people who live in a very different sociocultural context. Invite them to show you barriers, lack of perception, and oversights that will prohibit you from creating spaces that support children's potential and aspirations.

How We Begin

To begin, see yourself as a seed endowed with growth intelligence. Within you lies the potential for growth and new life. In the right conditions, you can become new. You carry the substance and possibility to nourish and support the development of a new way forward. You can expand to liberate yourself, your family, and your community.

Here's a fun fact: A seed that is planted upside down will grow in the right direction. Sensing gravity, the roots will grow downward into the soil, while the stem sprouts in the opposite direction. Like a seed, even if you feel upside down in the soil of antiracism—your schemata are shaped by unhealthy social conditions—you are designed to grow in the direction that bears fruit for justice and belonging. As a seed, consider your constitution, for example, social background, norms, and context, strengths, weaknesses, trauma, gains, and losses. Acknowledge where you are beginning and where you are planted. Be honest about where you are and how you feel about intentional growth. Identify your fears, apprehensions, and goals. Consider areas in your life where you have room to grow and what adjustments you will have to make. For example, contemplate making room in your life to take a series of antiracism education courses. Envision yourself as an antiracist, a colaborer in dismantling racist ideas and structures in your home, community, school, and classroom. If you are BIPOC, envision sharing the load with White people. Contrary to popular misunderstanding, our White peers and colleagues are not fragile. If you are White, envision carrying your weight alongside BIPOC. If you can raise a child or lead a classroom or a school, you can cultivate justice and belonging.

Reflection and Practice

REFLECTION

1. Describe your racial schemata. Growing up, did you talk about race/ism with adults at home or in school? If so, what did you talk about?

2. How are you socializing yourself, your children, and your classrooms about race? What conversations are you having with your children and students about who they are racially? What conversations would you like to have if you have not begun?

3. Identify changes that need to occur within your heart, home, classroom, or school that maintain old structures and practices that will not serve the new vision.

PRACTICE

1. Knowing your starting point will help you determine how to move forward. We have witnessed well-meaning parents, teachers, and education leaders jump into diversity, equity, and inclusion or antiracism initiatives without clarity about where or why they are starting. If a classroom teacher is ready to transform their curriculum to include multiple perspectives, but the students' parents resist this approach, growth will be compromised. Similarly, if a school leader is ready to shift school policies and practices to foster belonging and justice but classroom teachers are afraid to talk about race/ism, early growth will be stalled. Consider who, in your circle (including yourself), is ready (or not ready) to cultivate justice and belonging.

2. Create a list of how you will reduce your intrinsic and extraneous load. How will you maximize your germane load?

CHAPTER 4
ROOT: Build Racial Competency and Understanding

A people without knowledge of their past history, origin and culture is like a tree without roots.
—Marcus Garvey, Jamaican political activist

Roots are the lifeline of a plant. They provide an anchor so that the plant can resist the forces of wind and flow of water or mud. From the soil, the root system moves oxygen, water, and nutrients to the plant. Roots also stimulate and support microorganisms in the soil that benefit plant life and prevent soil erosion. In this chapter, we share ways to become anchored in antiracism so that you are empowered, committed, consistent, and persistent.

* * *

Amy, White Mom of Five
I have always been a bit of a history nerd: not the war, dates, and battlefield kind but rather the one who connects people to a place or home. I grew up watching *This Old House* on Saturday mornings and walking through Detroit's historic home tours with my parents. Connecting with my family and where we have lived has always

been important and interesting to me. So when I was reading Carol Anderson's book *White Rage: The Unspoken Truth of Our Racial Divide* (2016), I was surprised to hear a story that happened in Black Bottom, an area in Detroit that I had never heard of. This area was home to a large Black community in Detroit. It had hotels, bowling alleys, bars, swanky supper clubs, and a few greasy spoons. This area in the early 1900s was also home to many immigrant families before most of them moved out in the 1930s. It made me wonder where my family lived in Detroit at that time.

With the help of my dad, I started checking census records for my family's addresses. My family immigrated to the United States in the late 1800s and early 1920s from Germany. When I started to map out where my family lived in relation to Black Bottom, I realized that one set of my great-grandparents lived there. I was shocked. I had no idea that my history was also part of the history of this community. While doing this research I found redlined maps of Detroit. Redlining is the discriminatory practice of denying services (typically financial) to residents of certain areas based on their race or ethnicity. Black Bottom was designated red, and therefore Black people in this community could not get mortgages and had to rent dilapidated apartments and homes—sometimes with multiple families. This made it impossible for them to gain equity and save for owning their own home. However, the census revealed to me that my White great-grandparents did own their own home and were able to move to a nicer area of town not long after living in Black Bottom.

Because my great-grandparents were able to move within the city, this made it possible for my grandparents and parents to move out of the city and into the suburbs. They could not have done this if they had not been able to accrue some wealth through home-ownership. My White immigrant family was given access to many resources in the city that Black families who had lived in the city for generations were not able to get and would take years to acquire. I had to start seeing the history of my family through the lens of systemic racism and how they benefited from that very system. They were able to assimilate into Whiteness and therefore were able to live in a way that their Black counterparts were not allowed. I have great respect for my ancestors and all that they accomplished but it would be wrong not to see their stories in light of all the other stories lived—stories of exclusion, segregation, hatred, and even violence.

While I was now seeing my story impacted by race and immigration policies from a bird's-eye view, I turned the lens inward on my own heart and mind. I was trying to be more aware of my own internal bias and bring it out into the open so that I could change the ways I had been conditioned to think of others. I started at Target.

One day, pulling into the parking lot, I noticed a Black woman dressed really chic with great shoes and a handbag. Instantly I thought, "How did she get that?"

Whoa! Where did that come from? I had to admit that part of me was jealous and that I didn't really believe that this woman was worthy of having those things if I didn't have them myself. I call this internalized thinking *racist ugly*. I have hundreds of *racist ugly* moments that happen daily that I could share. I know that we are able as human beings to make new paths in our brains and change the way we think. I wanted to try out an experiment. So I went back to Target.

As I walked around Target and saw a Black person in the aisle, I would smile and say in my head, *You are my family*. For me, family is very important. Family is who you root for, who you love, who you protect and care for, who you advocate for, who you laugh with and see fully. So I would go to the next aisle and do the same thing: see a Black person and say in my head, *You are my family*. After doing this many times on different trips to stores, I felt my heart change. I realized that I had not been truly seeing other people as simply my siblings. "You are my family" has truly changed me.

* * *

Recall the teacher leader we mentioned in Chapter 1, who wanted measurable outcomes or fruit without the benefit of growing a root structure. Roots are the lifeline of a plant or tree. Without a strong root system, trees have no anchor, cannot mature to bear fruit, and cannot withstand adverse winds. Furthermore, roots are a place to store nutrients during times of drought, heat, cold, and virus. When we don't invest in developing a healthy root structure, we potentially set ourselves up to experience several setbacks and backslide when challenges come our way.

For cultivating justice and belonging, developing a healthy root structure entails understanding contributing systemic injustice and exclusionary policies and practices. For example, when we have working knowledge of how and why our communities, schools, classrooms, and districts became racially segregated and how they can consistently perpetuate inequality, we know where to enact change. Building racial competency is key to developing a root structure. Amy's story is a great example of how to examine your root structure.

Dr. Ali Michael (2016) of the Penn Center for the Study of Race and Equity in Education defines racial competence as having the skill and attitude required to do the following:

1. Develop and maintain healthy cross-racial relationships
2. Notice and analyze racial dynamics
3. Confront racism in the environment and in oneself

Although we are all racialized or socialized into racial groups, most of us are not encouraged to become racially competent. In fact, within the colorblind or race-blind framework, we are not allowed or equipped to recognize the historical social context that informs our current circumstances. Building racial competence allows us to understand, for example, how many of us continue to live in segregated neighborhoods several decades after President Lyndon B. Johnson signed the Civil Rights Act of 1965, which legally ended the segregation institutionalized by Jim Crow laws, and the Fair Housing Act of 1968, which ended discrimination in renting and selling homes.

Building racial competency does not have to feel like walking through a land mine wrought with heated debate and explosive discussions as is often anticipated. Amy began as a participant in an introductory-level onboarding course. The course, What LIES Between Us–Fostering First Steps Toward Racial Healing (Berry, 2016) was designed to equip learners with history, context, and an analytical framework for examining race/ism in the United States. Course modules guide learners on a journey to discover the roles that pseudoscience, false narratives (or "lies" as implied in the course title), public policies, immigration, racial ignorance, and brain bias played in inventing, normalizing, and maintaining the concept of race and racial inequity.

Ultimately, in this course, Amy was equipped with a historical, political, and social context for understanding race/ism and how it is sustained. Through the educational content and reflective practices, she was able to build a sound knowledge base and expand her perspective beyond the popular uninformed, anecdotal conversations around racism. For example, in understanding that people are not inherently a "race" but over time are racialized, learners are more eager to abdicate from adhering to racist ideology as natural. Instead, they ascribe to dismantling contrived racial misconceptions and injustice. By the end of the course, learners—BIPOC and White—express being both disturbed and relieved to understand the pervasive, systemic modality of racism. In other words, though racism has shaped systems and mindsets, both can be transformed. During the course, because their racial experiences are viewed within a factual, historical context, some African American learners have expressed they feel seen and validated. Most White learners are grateful to uncover what had been hidden from them by White supremacy ideology, meritocracy, denial, and colorblindness. One White male student notably shared that he felt "corrected and respected."

During the What LIES Between Us course, after learning a great deal of history regarding the beliefs, policies, and practices that solidified race into our national conscience, *Chapter Six - Disrupting Lies, Living Truth* of the study guide asks learners, "Where do you see yourself in the race story?" Amy then took the responsibility to learn how the history of immigration and racist policies formed social and economic mobility for her own family. Learning how policies inform practice and behavior equipped Amy with a critical lens. She clearly saw how her great-grandparents were invited to belong to an expanding economic opportunity, while their proximate African American peers were intentionally excluded. Amy took the responsibility to engage in heart work. She acknowledged how government sanctioned segregation shaped her perception of Black people. Though often subconscious, conformity to racist ideology dehumanizes us. Because she was honest with herself, she was able to address harmful biases and transform her thinking. In doing so, she restored her own humanity. Amy is an informed and empowered decision-maker. Her motivation for change is understood within our collective national story.

Our efforts to heal ourselves, our schools, and communities must be relational and transformative, not trendy or transactional. Our motivation and actions have to extend beyond the performance of displaying a stack of books featuring BIPOC lead characters or written by BIPOC authors. We cannot be satisfied with diversity in media representation or a racially diverse student population. If you are engaging in cultivating justice and belonging simply because it feels like the right thing to do or it is popular, as soon as you experience resistance from a peer, parent, or teacher you will find it easier to quit.

When you begin to see and understand how racism as an ideology and institution has shaped public policy and personal practices, the next step is to find your personal story within the story. It may be challenging to understand how race-based and immigration policies and social practices shaped your life, but awareness is necessary for your freedom. Think about when you pose for a group photo. When you look at the photo, where do you look first? You look at yourself first. You take account of how you look. Likewise, when we see the picture of our nation's history of structural racial injustice, we must zoom in and look at ourselves within the racialized context. For example, when people fail to examine Whiteness as an arbitrarily determined identity, they subsequently fail to view racism as belonging to White bodies and White spaces but instead perceive it to be a Black problem. Understanding that racism, though crippling to everyone, is a product of Whiteness is fundamental to knowing what needs to be dismantled.

When first realizing the truth about the racist and exclusionary policies and practices of the United States, it is tempting to dismiss it as a bygone era where "those White people back then did those things, which we no longer do." But when we see ourselves in the picture as heirs of their choices, we are able to make connections. We see how we live in and with the choices they made. We see how we've been shaped by their ideas and practices. We understand that we do not have to perpetuate their errors. We feel empowered to make different choices. If they were able to create systems that harmed people, certainly we are able to create systems and practices that cherish people.

As we explore racial identity or learn about our racial selves, we ask: Who am I as a raced person? How do I connect to my race? Socialization feeds our racial selves. Therefore, we can ask: How have inside forces (family, friends, parents), and outside forces (media, books, acquaintances, strangers) shaped what I believe about myself and others? As Beverly Tatum shares in her book *Why Are All the Black Kids Sitting Together in the Cafeteria?* (1997/2017), we have been socialized to believe things about racial others that are often stereotypical, and most times incomplete. If we live in racially homogeneous communities, we get secondhand information about racial groups via the news or social media or the story from our friend's babysitter's husband. If we don't have any factual knowledge or lived experience in our schemata to challenge the information, such stories resonate as true. So ask yourself: Where are my roots in my racial schemata?

As you notice and analyze racial dynamics, past and present, you will experience cognitive dissonance, which may feel uncomfortable. But discomfort due to growth is good. Take the time to examine your discomfort. Examine the source. For example, if you feel defensive, ask yourself why. What is triggering you? What are you afraid of? What happens after this moment can either allow you to develop your roots or stunt your growth. We see this discomfort pushing back on a national stage through the manufactured fear and debate around critical race theory (CRT) and book banning. The murder of George Floyd by Derek Chauvin violently shook our country and the world in a way that awakened a realization of our collective humanity. Corporations, small businesses, churches, school districts, and homes committed themselves to identifying and changing harmful and oppressive practices, and engaged in learning about race/ism. We believe that the massive movement toward antiracism education and antiracist action occurred too rapidly for some people, who saw this movement as forced transparency, increased accountability, and ultimately, a threat to their social power. We believe that fear filled the chasm between growth toward antiracism and complicity with the racial status quo.

Author and scholar Carol Anderson attributes this type of forward movement backlash to what she calls White rage. In a 2021 Vox interview, Dr. Anderson expressed, "When Black Americans in particular make strides toward equality, the determined hand of White supremacy pushes back." White supremacy is the ideology that White people and the ideas, thoughts, beliefs, and actions of White people are superior to people of color and their ideas, thoughts, beliefs, and actions. There are people who truly believe that White people are inherently superior; therefore, BIPOC liberation and progress feels like a threat to their existence. Anderson (2016) writes in her book *White Rage:*

> The trigger for White rage, inevitably, is Black advancement. It is not the mere presence of Black people that is the problem; rather, it is blackness with ambition, with drive with purpose, with aspirations, and with demands for full and equal citizenship. (p. 3)

She argues that White rage has been used since the formation of the United States and aligns directly with White supremacy. White rage violently erupts to preserve White status and power.

We've seen this type of retaliation with the recent anti-CRT state legislation. As young and old people en masse began to examine the social and economic infrastructure that benefits some and dispossesses others, those who felt threatened frantically rushed to influence policies. The ban of CRT in states through legislative acts began with one bill, which was then copied, pasted, and passed along state by state. The anti-CRT bills restrict schools, districts, and universities from teaching or talking about diversity, race, racism, and antiracism, under the guise that White students will feel bad about being White. Each state lists their own terms and lessons that cannot be taught. Fortunately, many students, teachers, and families have advocated for antiracism initiatives in schools. Let's not be stalled by White rage or any other resistance to forward movement. Search your beliefs and ideas about race to eliminate any and all notions of White supremacy and resistance to BIPOC advancement.

Also, as you notice and analyze racial dynamics and examine racial identity, you may feel troubled or even enraged by what you learn. When such feelings show up, honor them by allowing yourself to feel them. Refuse to repress and separate yourself from unwanted feelings by surrendering to defense mechanisms such as guilt, denial, and rationalization. These unpleasant feelings are not telling you to retreat. They are telling you that this is important. Anneliese Singh (2019) shares in *Racial Healing Handbook* that we need to grieve racism. Racism happened, is happening, and will continue to happen until we are able to name it and grieve the harm it caused and continues to cause. Grieve, but do not linger into shame—for not knowing it all, or for having made mistakes, or for having White advantage and access.

Tehia

I remember reading James Loewen's 1995 book *Lies My Teacher Told Me* for the first time in graduate school. I was blown away. I was furious about how there were so many gaps and holes in what I was taught in my K–12 education. Loewen's book helped me see more of the full picture. In Amy's story at the beginning of this chapter, she knew a lot about "her" Detroit, but not the whole story of Detroit. The perspective of Black people's experiences was missing. Like Amy, I sought multiple perspectives to broaden my understanding. Schools can do a much better job at providing multiple perspectives so that students can explore multiple experiences of a situation and not have to do it in adulthood.

I distinctly remember learning about Native Americans in elementary school: how they were savages and lived in tepees and how Thanksgiving was a great celebration of the Pilgrims and Indians coming together to celebrate the harvest. I also remember making and wearing a headdress at school. It would be 30 years before I learned a historically accurate narrative about Indigenous people. I did three things:

1. I read Roxanne Dunbar-Ortiz's (2014) book *An Indigenous People's History of the United States*. What a different story from the one I was taught in elementary school.
2. I watched PBS specials and documentaries on Native Americans.
3. I developed cross-racial relationships with Native people like a former doctoral student who is Lumbee: Dr. Brittany D. Hunt, who also has a great TED talk on *Indigenous Resilience* (2020).

Because I didn't want to add to the emotional labor of Indigenous friends by having them inform me of what I should know, number three was a bit more difficult. Notice that I engaged with a colleague with whom I had a healthy relationship, not with an acquaintance that I didn't really know. Personally, I know how it feels to be asked 50 questions from a person who did no self-exploration or from strangers. Being seen as the primary resource for "teach me everything about Black people, Black History Month, food, and hair" is exhausting.

To expand my roots, I looked for scholars and voices of color who were experts by lived experience or by their research. I prioritized and read the research, publications, and creative works produced by Indigenous people. I searched for asset-oriented content and critiqued deficit-oriented content. Asset orientation acknowledges and identifies the resilience and contributions of a person or group despite the oppressive conditions. Deficit orientation victimizes people by primarily identifying them as the negative outcome of social and economic injustice. Deficit language may include words like *minority, disadvantaged, at risk*, and others that victimize a racial group versus discussing their strengths. Deficit language also does not address the systems that may have caused a people group to be disadvantaged or at risk. There are scholars who use deficit-oriented language within their work. I decided not to use such resources.

As I read and learned, I generated lists of questions to ask and connections I made. I call this practice the Dinner Party Scenario. When invited to a dinner party, it's normal to bring something for the meal or a gift to show gratitude to the host. Similarly, when we want to learn about people who are different from us and want to know more from a representative of that group, we should bring something to the table to show gratitude for the host. Here are some ways to bring something to the table:

1. Do your homework. Read books, listen to podcasts, and watch documentaries created by people in that racial group.
2. Take notes and write down your questions. Then try to answer the questions with the resources you have.

3. When you cannot find the answer, those are the questions you might ask your trusted person with whom you are already in community.

Come to the table having done some of the heavy lifting. Do not come to the table asking that person to do all the work for you. We want to reduce their racial battle fatigue, not increase it. Don't expect people to feed you when you are capable of feeding yourself. Some of the information you've acquired may be incorrect, but those who sit at the table with you will show you grace because you came to the table prepared and are already in relationship with them.

I moved beyond the mindset of "I don't want to say the wrong thing," because that fear bound me to potentially saying nothing at all. Silence is harmful and expensive. I chose to put myself out there and lead with vulnerability. In her 2019 Netflix special *The Call to Courage,* Brené Brown says to "choose courage over comfort." She adds that vulnerability is critical for connections and relationships and even for businesses to flourish. I came to the table prepared, curious, and genuinely interested. I chose to be vulnerable and courageous because I wanted to understand deeper.

Ultimately, I was furious that as a child I was misinformed and deprived of knowing the brilliance, history, and dignity of Native American people in elementary school. We didn't address colonization and the savagery of the White colonists via murder, lies within the treaties, and the trauma invoked on First Nation families through boarding schools like Carlisle Boarding School, where founder, Richard Pratt's mantra was "Kill the Indian. Save the Man." I didn't learn about affirming Native American history. I was hurt that when I became a teacher, I then retaught to my elementary students. Sometimes I wake up in a cold sweat thinking about how I taught misinformation about entire nations of people to children. Since I have learned so much more, I have made it my mission to continue to learn and teach accurate Native American history. Now that I know better, I do better.

When I teach undergraduate teacher candidates, I spend a significant amount of time helping them understand the complexities and nuances of race/ism and consider pedagogical approaches to convey the information. I use children's literature by authors of color or other authors who write from a historically accurate perspective. I teach them to examine stories used for Thanksgiving and discuss how to replace anecdotal myths with precise information. As I work with teachers, I help them understand the harm of teaching the Pilgrims and Indians fairytale. If they need help with more accurate content, I am happy to supply the books, websites, videos and come in and use those resources. The books and language I use in my 5-year-old's classroom are age-appropriate. While I do consider my audience—children, college students, teaching adults and parents—I do not sugarcoat what happened to Indigenous people in this country.

Fortunately, our children are much more sophisticated in their thinking than we give them credit for. They can handle painful truths. We've heard adults say that by hiding painful truths from our children, we are preserving their innocence. However, when we erase the culture, lives, brilliance, contributions, love, conflict, suffering, and entire human experience of people groups, we teach our children that people are expendable—that some people must be thrown away so that other people, in this case colonizers, can thrive. What we are actually preserving is a scarcity mindset. It's more cognitively congruent to learn the whole story or history than to have to unlearn all the inaccuracies, and then relearn historically accurate information. And the great news is that we don't have to wait until National Native American Heritage Month (November); we can do this year-round.

As a parent and teacher, I want to be a critical consumer of information. When considering what to teach our children and students, we debate breadth versus depth. While breadth allows me to teach a wide range of content, with depth I can focus on a specific topic and drill down into the content. The same is applicable for me. I don't have to know everything, but I should be prepared to lead children and for the 50 million questions they ask as they try to make sense of their world.

How to Become Rooted

The first step in becoming rooted is to accept that building racial competency and understanding takes more time and effort than a 1-day workshop or lecture can afford. Although there are powerful learning experiences that are designed for 1- or 2-day settings, our bodies are not capable of doing all of the digesting, processing, thinking, reflecting, unlearning, realigning, reimagining, and creating required to establish strong roots in antiracism. Like learning a new language, our brain has to construct a new schema or cognitive framework. And because learning requires sustained, consistent practice, we need time. When we grow slow, we grow deep.

Like Amy, embrace a growth mindset. Seek to understand how race-specific and immigration policies impacted where you grew up and where you currently live. Be curious and open to learning about how institutionalized segregation impacted your family of origin and shaped your perspective. If you are a teacher or teacher leader, learn what role community policies, zoning, and funding played in determining your school's population.

In a few instances, parents and teachers at historically or predominantly White private schools have asked us why families of color are not attracted to their schools, don't feel welcome there, or why the retention rate for students of color is so low. One leader asked, "How can we grow more diverse, if our Black families keep leaving the school?" They blamed the lack of racial diversity on Black families either not enrolling or leaving. We invited them to ask different questions:

- ◆ Did the school's founders create the school specifically as a White space?
- ◆ Does the location of the school impact access and enrollment?
- ◆ Do services provided (or not provided) restrict who can attend? For example, are lunch and transportation provided?
- ◆ What efforts have school leaders and investors taken to desegregate the school?
- ◆ What efforts has the school community made to create a culture where historically excluded families now belong?
- ◆ Do school policies (teacher, student, school handbook) protect the dignity of everyone as opposed to centering White racial norms?
- ◆ As a historically White institution, have you identified and omitted curricula and practices that center White identity?
- ◆ Have you instituted curricula and practices that reflect BIPOC perspectives, history, stories, and lived experiences?

Perhaps families of color do not perceive that particular school as a place where their children will be safe or thrive. The school leader wanted to racially diversify the student population, but was the school willing to create a school where families of color feel seen, valued, and safe? Families of color are not mere transactions for the sake of a "diversity" trend. Families of color want roots in a school as well. No one wants to move from school to school but will do what it takes to find the right fit. All students, including White students, benefit from environments that wholly value and nurture them completely.

As a parent, understand that you may need to equip your children with a different racial toolkit than the one you had. Commit to finding your own personal story within our nation's racial story. Understand ways your social identity has been determined by public policies. If you grew up in racially segregated spaces—neighborhoods, schools, churches—consider whose stories were excluded. How often did you read books or watch movies and shows in which BIPOC were main characters who were not fighting for basic human rights? Look for, listen to, and learn from lived experiences that were considered intrinsically different from your own. Then do the same thing for your children. We can help them develop roots far sooner than we did.

Write your story. Read your story. Analyze your story. Notice where you see a learning deficit, cognitive dissonance, and potential for growth. Acknowledge wins and insights. As you build racial competence, you grow your capacity to see and analyze racial dynamics, engage in active antiracism, and develop and maintain healthy cross-racial relationships. As parents and teachers, we often worry about how we can move beyond colorblindness and nurture our children's natural curiosity without perpetuating a racial hierarchy. James Baldwin said, "Children have never been very good at listening to their elders, but they have never failed to imitate them" (1961). Our children are watching us. Your competence will lead to confident, healthy, life-giving lessons and conversations with your children that foster a healthy racial identity. Your children will learn implicitly and explicitly as you engage them in normalized racial awareness, understanding, critical thinking, and problem-solving. Those roots will grow deeper, and stronger.

Becoming Rooted Together

Working together is exponentially better than working alone. For this reason, we work with teachers and parents in cohorts. Connect with parents or teachers who are doing, or at least trying to do, what you are doing. Your colaborer does not have to be proximate to your neighborhood or school or within your family. You can build community with teachers at other schools and parents in other neighborhoods. Social media and other online spaces can be a great resource for building community. Along with our peers and colleagues, we have created the Anti-Racism Collective (ARC) at University of North Carolina (UNC) Charlotte (with Dr. Erin Miller) and Brownicity—Many Hues One Humanity, an education agency dedicated to making important, scholarly informed, antiracism education accessible to the public through designed curricula and courses, curated lessons, and consulting. We bring teachers and parents together to learn and grow together while supporting and encouraging each other.

In 2015, Dr. Miller and I (Tehia) realized that our teacher candidates needed more support in working with racially diverse students. Teachers were also requesting support in connecting with their racially diverse students. From those requests, conversations, presentations, and publications, we dreamt and created the antiracism graduate certificate program at UNC Charlotte. It is a 12-credit graduate certificate program that is 100 percent online so we could connect with as many adults as we could. The four courses in the program focus intentionally and specifically on antiracism in the fields, industries, or interests of our students: (1) History and Psychology of Racism; (2) Racial Identity Development; (3) Race in Education and Schooling; and (4) Anti-Racism Activism. It began as a program for teachers and quickly expanded its student base as more diverse industries and fields began to enroll in the program.

We have our students evaluate our courses annually to ensure we are providing the content they need to expand their roots in content and connection. Since 2017, we have had hundreds of students graduate from the program, which expands the network of other adults who are committed to antiracism, and we developed the Anti-Racism Collective as a way to organize anyone who is interested in antiracism in their spheres of influence.

As you look for opportunities to develop and maintain healthy cross-racial relationships, consider where you play, worship, work, shop, and serve. Courageously expand your circle by moving in different circles. In her 2017 book *On Intersectionality*, Kimberlé Crenshaw introduced intersectionality as a way to view the whole of peoples' identity. Envision your dinner party table filled with friends diversified by race, ethnicity, culture, gender, sexual identity, sexual orientation, language, ability, religion, citizenship, socioeconomic status, and family structure contributing multiple perspectives and offering an expanded knowledge base. You all are committed to learning together—not just so you can feel good about yourself but also ultimately to normalize diversity for our children so that they have the capacity to foster justice and belonging.

We strongly believe that much of this growth needs to take place in communities and spaces that are culturally and racially heterogeneous. However, we understand that there are times when an affinity space is needed to address the specific needs of that group. Affinity groups are the informal or formal organizing of people who have shared backgrounds or interests. For example, we noticed that after each Brownicity meeting, White team members huddled together to grieve over how they had been criticized and ostracized by a family member or longtime friend for disavowing White entitlement. And Black parents whose children attend predominantly White schools sometimes huddle in the school parking lot to affirm each other's experiences. Be sure to offer space, if necessary, to groups to meet separately away from the larger or perhaps dominant racial group. Affinity groups should be given equal time, attention, and resources as the collective group.

For Parents and Educators of Color to Consider

When you are called upon to lead, you are not obligated to be everything for everyone. Set your boundaries. Know your value and worth. We are often asked and expected to do all of the heavy lifting. Also, we are asked and expected to do all of the heavy lifting without acknowledgment or compensation. While we may choose to lead our communities to freedom, we are not slaves. When you are invited to use your personal and professional experiences to add value to a learning experience, curriculum, event, lesson plan, workshop, or anything that you did not volunteer to do, expect compensation. People, corporations, communities, and districts need to normalize sowing into those they are asking to lead or contribute.

In a capitalist economy such as ours, compensation should be money. Unfortunately, in a capitalist economy such as ours, education is severely underfunded, so sometimes money is not available. Compensation can be resources, time off, release from another obligation, or something else you propose. If compensation is not offered, ask for it. If you are denied, specifically outline what you are willing to do and what you don't have the capacity to do. For example, a teacher of color needed help creating boundaries because as one of the few teachers of color at her school, she was being exploited by an administrator. The administrator wanted this teacher to lead and run the diversity, equity, and inclusion (DEI) committee. The teacher was denied when she asked for compensation. The teacher told the administrator to give her a day to think about what she wanted to do. The next day, the teacher then created a list (i.e., boundaries) of what she would and would not do. She agreed to lead the DEI teacher workshop but chose not to do all the work that goes into organizing it like gathering supplies, sending invitations and reminders, and coordinating the lunch plans. The administrator agreed to those terms because the teacher was able to articulate that she was already overextended with other committees. In another instance, educators have agreed to curate the resources but not teach the content to their colleagues.

If there is no value, people will not invest. Cultivating justice and belonging is valuable and worthwhile toil. There must be an investment. Expect an investment. If people refuse to invest in some way, consider that they are asking you to sow seed into rocky soil. In the Sower of Seed parable in the Bible (Matthew 13), rocky soil represents people who are initially enthusiastic but have no deep roots or investment, thus no long-term commitment. And when people are not anchored to and invested, they abandon the growth process when challenges come.

When you need to say no to being exploited, here are a few phrases you can use:

- Thanks for inviting me to participate/lead; however. . . .
- My plate is currently full with _____ obligations.
- All my service obligations have been fulfilled.
- I don't have the bandwidth for _____.
- I must leave at __ time; therefore, I am unable to __.
- No thank you.

We also understand that there are power dynamics at play. If you feel like you cannot say no to an administrator or leader, think about how the imposed responsibility can be used to either elevate your trajectory or make connections with someone who can. Do these uncompensated roles show up on your resume? Can you consider being nominated for an award because of the work you are doing or nominated for program you are interested in? Often the awards or prestigious programs are another way to be rewarded for your work.

While supporting your school, home, or organization can be exhilarating, the heavy lifting can also be exhausting. William Smith coined the term *racial battle fatigue*, and described it as the cumulative effect of enduring microaggressions, discrimination, and blatant racism on a regular basis. Fasching-Varner, Albert, Mitchell, and Allen (2015) expand racial battle fatigue in the context of higher education in their book *Racial Battle Fatigue in Higher Education*, but their conclusions apply to K–12 classrooms as well. The reality is we don't have the luxury of escaping racism. Therefore, we have to take care of ourselves. One way to take care of yourself is by protecting your intellectual property.

We know that colleagues and friends are going to ask for help and accountability. In these instances, protect your intellectual property. Unfortunately, co-opting and appropriating the ideas and work of BIPOC is common. Remember, investing in antiracism is not yet seen as necessary and normal. Consider ways to protect your work. Make sure your name is on everything you create. Because a meme can go viral in a moment's notice, be sure that your name, logo, or watermark appear on it. In meetings when you propose an idea, make sure your contribution is noted or acknowledged. If you are considering the risk, be sure you include it on your annual report, evaluation, and resume. For too long, BIPOC's work has gone unacknowledged and unrewarded, which is unacceptable in a just and belonging environment.

Also, radical self-care is necessary! It is your responsibility to take care of yourself before you take care of others. Even the airlines tell us we have to put the oxygen mask on ourselves before we put one on someone else. From maternal death rates and state-sanctioned murder to food deserts, COVID-19, and internal and external stressors, racism is killing us. As Bettina Love (2019) shares in her book *We Want to Do More Than Survive,* our goal is to thrive, not just survive. Love charges us to be well so we can continue to dream about and work toward a better world for ourselves and our legacies. Implement a self-care plan. What can you do to take care of yourself for 5 minutes, 30 minutes, 1 hour, 3 hours, 6 hours, and 24 hours? Create a list that fits in those categories and a self-care plan document to detail what you can do (Appendix B). Put your care plan on your calendar and stick to it like any other appointment. Try to enact self-care at least once a week. If you don't have a therapist and can afford one, get one. In the meantime, access the Liberate app, created by BIPOC for BIPOC. The app offers a diverse array of meditations and teachers to choose from.

For White Parents and Teachers to Consider

As we said earlier, begin with self-reflection. What do you know? Where are your gaps? Have you noticed a pattern when you are around BIPOC? Who are you biased toward? When does your racial stamina begin to fade? When you are around BIPOC, are you comfortable or uncomfortable? Is it location or context specific? Is your body settled? Are you ready for the cognitive dissonance or discomfort that comes along with this work? These are questions that need to be answered before and while you prepare to engage with others. Resmaa Menakem shares:

> If you're white, you may discover that when you can settle and manage your body, you won't feel a need to manage Black ones—or a need to ask Black ones to manage yours. You'll also be better able to manage, challenge, and disrupt white-body supremacy. (p. 152)

As you actively and intentionally develop and maintain healthy cross-racial relationships, be mindful of your methods for getting to know BIPOC. Be careful that your getting-to-know-you phase does not come across like interrogation. Nor should it feel like speed dating—asking 20 questions. In the first few seconds of being approached by a White person, we have been asked questions like, "What neighborhood do you live in?" "Where do you work?" "What do you do?" This type of questioning feels less like relationship building blocks and more like inquiry of suspicion, as if you are working to confirm or dispel any stereotypes or beliefs you hold. Interrogation builds walls, not relationships. Getting to know someone organically and building relationships takes time. Observe, listen, lean in, and breathe.

Also, be mindful to pull your own weight. We need you to see and understand your Whiteness so that you don't harm BIPOC. Ultimately, we don't need you to be allies. Allyship is passive and does not require action. Allyship is also self-designated, which means you decided you were an ally. But would your BIPOC colleagues agree with your self-designated title? We need you well. We need you to be antiracists, committed to disrupting harmful systems, practices, and beliefs. We need action-oriented and invested collaboration. We need you to take the responsibility to create spaces and classrooms where all children are valued and can thrive. We need you to not be asleep at the wheel while you raise your children at home and have charge over ours in the community. We need you to be willing to disrupt injustice when BIPOC are not in the room. We need you to ask:

- How do I engage my White colleagues in cultivating justice and belonging?
- How can I support my colleagues of color?
- When do I speak up for people who are not at the table and when do I invite them to the table or create space at the table to speak for themselves?

Instead of looking for BIPOC in your group to affirm your growth, set your aperture for self-praise. You are becoming antiracist for the sake of cultivating justice and belonging for all, not to receive praise or favor from anyone, nor to prove that you are not a racist. Don't place the burden on others to acknowledge your growth. Celebrate yourself. And if friends choose to celebrate you, then be sure to appreciate and celebrate them as well. The synergy is contagious.

Individually and collectively, we anchor ourselves in antiracism, not only to bear the fruit of justice and belonging but also to withstand adversity. Rooted, together we can heal ourselves and our communities. We can then grow our capacity to imagine and manifest spaces where racial harm is the exception and no longer embedded within institutions and behavioral norms.

Reflection and Practice
REFLECTION
>   1. Consider how your personal story has been shaped and formed by the larger story of race/ism and immigration.
>   2. How are you equipping your children or students to not impose racial harm on their peers of color?
>   3. Parents and teachers of color, how does racial battle fatigue show up in your life?

PRACTICE
>   1. If you, like Amy, are aware of how systems have impacted you, consider what you need to do next to nurture your root structure. Who can hold you accountable?
>   2. Consider your dinner party scenario. Generate a list of questions you are ready to get answers to, try to find the answers, then ask your trusted person the questions you couldn't answer.
>   3. For teachers, look at a part of your unit, standards, or instruction guide for the year. Whose story is told, and whose is missing?

CHAPTER 5
SPROUT: Early Growth and Signs of Hope

The stem of greatness sprouts from the seed of sacrifice.
—Kedar Joshi, Astrologer

A s the roots anchor the seed within the soil, a small plant begins to emerge and breaks through. This is the sprout. The sprout is a testament of the successful coalescence of soil, seed, and roots. The sprout is the beginning of recognizable and measurable growth. Some seeds, like peas, radishes, and watermelon, sprout in days, whereas other plants can take years to push through the soil. Artichokes can take over 2 years to show signs of growth and asparagus up to 6. While we still have more growing to do, the sprout indicates that we are, in fact, growing.

Before we share our stories of sprouting, we want to make you aware of something that inevitably stalls growth. We've witnessed this time and time again: the refusal to decenter or reprioritize White Anglo-Saxon Protestant (WASP), patriarchal, colonial settler, Manifest Destiny contrived tellings of history. We understand that a skewed, Eurocentric version of history was standardized for consumption in schools. However, we have the opportunity to teach content that is more historically accurate. We've watched parents and teachers resist this opportunity to expand as they've quoted this at us: "History is always written by the winners."

A quick Google search of this quote revealed that this theory was advanced by Leigh Teabing, who was later found to be unreliable and mentally unbalanced. Teabing surmised that when two or more cultures fight, the loser is obliterated, and the winner writes the history—stories that glorify their own cause and disparage the conquered.

The holes in this winner-takes-all theory are harmful and numerous. First, all intercultural communications and interactions are not necessarily conflict based. Though we are oversaturated in our understanding of colonization, not all people groups felt the need to conquer and dispossess others to survive. Also, recorded historical accounts of African and Indigenous civilizations that existed long before and alongside Europe are available and accessible. Choices have been made to deliberately exclude those lived experiences, contributions, advancements, and culture. Furthermore, prioritizing European and Western conquests, colonization, and contributions as normative behavior reinforces violence as a method of cultural cohabitation. And in doing so, we place a higher value on European and Western people and ideas and render those they exploited and oppressed as a necessary consequence. In other words, education has been used to teach how to esteem White people and how to devalue BIPOC.

As we challenge fixed ideas about history, we inevitably have to deconstruct our racial, cultural, and ethnic identities. While it may cause cognitive dissonance and be painful, deconstructing from harmful norms is good for us. Centering excluded voices and stories is essential to cultivating justice and belonging in all of our spaces. BIPOC contributions, resistance to oppression, liberatory actions, joy, and ordinary daily existence are American history and whose presence must be normalized in the teaching of American history. Remember, diversity only seems alternative within a White supremacy modality. In reality, diversity is quite normal. Learning something new and unlearning something old may cause discomfort. But don't allow a weed of resistance to spring up and choke out your potential.

Lucretia

Because we are an interracial couple, my husband anticipated our children would field many inquiries about their racial identity and experiences. We also understood that we—a Black woman and a White man—would need to give our multiethnic children different tools from the ones given to us to navigate our hyperracialized society.

My husband, Nathan (Nate), was born and raised in the small town of Indianola, Iowa, where he had little lived experience with people who were not White. His father pastored a rural church that literally had corn growing on three sides of the building. After Nate finished elementary school, his family moved to the city of Des Moines, Iowa, where his dad pastored a racially diverse church whose mission was to bridge ethnic, cultural, and denominational divides. Nate says that at the time he didn't know what *ethnic* or *diversity* meant.

I, on the other hand, was born and raised in the South in Winston-Salem, North Carolina. Desegregation laws had been in place for several years before I was born in a segregated Black hospital in 1971. While my formal life (school and work) was racially integrated, my familiar life (home, neighborhood, and church) remained segregated. Our neighborhood, once predominantly White, went through a period of White flight shortly after we moved in. Moving in and out of spaces that still bore the markings of Jim Crow segregation required me to be well informed about how race/ism works in our lives.

My husband and I met while attending Iowa State University, where I was in graduate school. Our friendship developed as we worked to racially integrate a campus ministry. When we married and anticipated having children, we intentionally had conversations about race, racial and ethnic identity, opportunities for growth, and challenges our multiethnic children might face. Nathan and I developed a lens and framework for how to address and educate them about the fallacy of race as biology and the realities of racism as a social practice. We wanted them to understand the racialized society in which we live while also equipping them to thrive in it and help change it for the better.

Within the loving, just, and belonging space of our family, race did not matter, race did not segregate us, nor did it mandate more opportunities for Nathan and dispossess me. But we did not pretend that we lived in a postracial society. As soon as our first child articulated our skin tones as different, we took time to expand her vocabulary and understanding. As a preschooler, she observed that we are all shades of brown: "Daddy is light brown, mommy is dark brown, and I am medium brown," she announced.

We expanded her understanding by teaching her about melanin, ancestry, and how skin color reflects her ancestor's geographic origins. Instead of reinforcing and conforming to the Black–White racial binary, we read nonfiction books and stories about skin color as various hues of brown. Later, when she was school-aged, we taught her about race/ism in a way that her young mind could process and understand it. We explained how and why rules were created to sort people into categories, called race, and how races were given abstract names: White, Black (historically, Negro). These race-based rules were established to benefit those racialized as White while unfairly depriving everyone else.

As we educated our children, we did not victimize or demonize people. We taught them to see the racial, social construct—defined by unfair rules—in which we live. Because as a family, we developed literacy, competence, and awareness, it has not been difficult to teach and learn the ugly history of racism or talk about current racism. We did not have one big conversation about race, where we downloaded four hundred years of history in one sitting. Consciousness, inquiry, and learning unfolded over a million small conversations contextualized within the moment. For example, as our daughter read the *Addie* series books (American Girl), we took the opportunity to expand her understanding of American chattel slavery and its connection to race/ism.

Some time later, as our daughter learned about Rev. Dr. Martin Luther King, Jr. and other civil rights activists in her kindergarten class, she needed more context to understand the need for their work. At that time, we taught her more about policies and practices that continued to shape advantages for White people and disadvantages for Black people. Two years later, when we began to officially celebrate Loving Day, we introduced her to the Loving story. Richard and Mildred Loving, an interracial couple, were married in 1958 in Washington, D.C., but when they returned home to Virginia, where interracial marriage was illegal, they were arrested. When she learned about miscegenation laws, which enforced racial segregation at the level of marriage and intimate relationships by criminalizing interracial marriage, our daughter became very upset. She yelled, "It's not fair that race laws say who gets to be born and who does not get to be born!" In that moment, I felt two things. Though my heart broke for her, I felt relieved that she was upset instead of indifferent about injustice. And I was awestruck that at 7 years old, she clearly understood race as a construct that determines lives and livelihood. Without me explicitly telling her, she realized that without the actions of the civil rights movement, she would not exist.

Our commitment to equipping our children with understanding and language came in handy when other families—many of them multiethnic by adoption or by marriage—began asking advice for how to address race. We found that parents were no longer willing to settle for the colorblind approach or oversimplified anecdotes regarding differences in skin color. However, parents did not feel competent and confident about integrating skin tone, phenotype, and race awareness and language into everyday life. "What if I say the wrong thing? I don't want to scar or scare my child," were the concerns we heard the most.

Because parents were both ready and cautious, I began cultivating a space where we could grow competent, conscious, and confident together. I called our learning community Brownicity to reflect the belonging and justice we wanted to foster. Brownicity is a hybrid word, formed by combining *Brown* and *ethnicity*. Brown represents melanin, the pigment we all have in our skin—darker skin tones have more, and lighter skin tones have less. In general, *ethnicity* is the concept of belonging to a social group that has commonalities. So *Brownicity*—the word and the agency—holds that though we've been racialized, all humans are a hue of brown. Essentially, as expressed through our tagline, we are *many hues but one humanity*. This framework set the intention and vision for fostering connection as we grew awareness of and de-aligned with divisive, racist ideas and narratives.

Brownicity launched with meetups attended by parents from various ethnic and racial backgrounds. Together we blossomed in our understanding of concepts and practices to help families navigate our racialized society in healthy ways and equip our children to thrive. Our common aspiration, willingness to learn, and commitment to action fortified our just and belonging space. We built community around a shared fundamental understanding of race/ism, a common language, and a mutual assertion to raise socially conscious—as opposed to racially colorblind—families. As we've grown into an official nonprofit education agency, Brownicity's mission is to foster education designed to create a shared understanding of race/ism to inspire a culture of true belonging and justice for all.

But even as a small group of parents and teachers, we gathered to address important practices like how to talk about, take care of, and honor various hair textures. During our Hair Affair event, we learned about and shared our favorite hair products most suitable for our various hair textures. We shared best methods and resources for normalizing conversations about skin tone and race. We also engaged in local learning opportunities like Racial Equity Institute's Dismantling Racism workshop. We attended events like Race—Are We So Different, a traveling exhibition that explores the science, history, and lived experience of race/ism in the United States, and Point Made Learning's *I'm Not Racist Am I?*, a feature documentary about how this next generation is going to confront racism. Committed to a journey, together we persistently took one action step at a time, one after another.

Our confidence and reach grew. A teacher and parent at our children's school invited me to lead a conversation with parents about how to talk about skin tone and race with our kids. I was amazed at the turnout. Parents showed up, brought their questions, and leaned in. They needed validation and encouragement to counter colorblind ideology, which they knew had deprived them and their children of basic understanding and context. They knew being silent about phenotypic differences and racism was not helpful but needed someone to affirm their intuition. We encouraged parents to start simple, build a foundation of understanding, and then grow from there. It is impossible to do all the work at once. Yes, some seeds, like lettuce, sprout quickly, but growing into antiracism is more like a carrot seed. It starts small and takes time.

Tehia

My family and I were reading a book at bedtime, and my 4-year-old son noticed that the characters in the story had brown skin like him, and he was excited about it. The work my partner and I had been doing to make sure our sons saw their brown skin as positive was paying off. However, I realize that simply repeating something will not be enough to make them proud to be young Black boys. We knew the work we had ahead of us, but it felt good to know that the seeds we planted to affirm their beautiful Blackness were beginning to sprout.

My own sprouting happened over time. Over the years, I became more aware of my Blackness and intentionally focused on it once I arrived at Bethune-Cookman for college. Being around the diversity of Black folks broadened my horizons in many ways. Learning about my history and the history of Bethune-Cookman founder Dr. Mary McLeod Bethune transformed my thoughts and understanding of myself and my people. My classmates were from across the globe—Florida, Georgia, Bahamas, Haiti, New York, Chicago, and of course San Diego. Our experiences—what we thought, how we talked, dressed, and ate—were different, and we appreciated each other for those differences. I realized that Black people are not a monolith.

I majored in elementary education, and after graduation I became a second-grade teacher. During my K–12 experiences, I didn't see myself in the curriculum or in the pedagogical approaches used in the classroom. There was no validation of my Blackness, or in the ways my teachers treated me. Therefore, I wanted to make sure my students had better schooling experiences where they had opportunities to see themselves in what they were learning in an affirming way. I wanted to instill in my students the same racial self-love that I acquired at Bethune-Cookman. While keeping within the required state standards, I tried to focus on Black history as much as possible. We took field trips to Bethune-Cookman, and I had my classmates and other city officials, newscasters, and other community members of color visit my classroom. I wanted my classroom guests to serve as mirrors for my students. They saw and heard from accomplished people who looked like them.

Revered scholar and author Rudine Sims Bishop (1990) shares that literature should be an opportunity for children to experience windows and mirrors in their world—mirrors in which they get to see themselves affirmed and as assets to the world and windows through which they get to see into lives, experiences, and communities that are different from their own. Books and media that are mirrors help children feel seen, heard, and valued. Meanwhile, windows help children broaden their perspectives. As we offer children windows and mirrors, we must be mindful to avoid reinforcing a deficit-oriented perspective of BIPOC characters and lived experiences. We need to provide young people with literature that goes beyond a Eurocentric purview. Instead we must offer windows into the assets, creativity, contributions, resilience, and joy of people in spite of colonization and oppressive systems.

Because I was struggling to find diverse books for my boys, I knew teachers would struggle as well. One of the projects I conducted focused on helping elementary teachers select books that were more racially diverse. I created a rubric for teachers to use as they selected books to use in their school and classroom (see Appendix C). I conducted a series of professional development (PD) sessions with teachers where we dedicated time to explore their school and classroom libraries. We looked at the populations of students who were in their class, moved beyond race, and looked at ethnicity and nationality. I pushed them beyond the category of *Asian* and explored resources to see that students were Vietnamese and Hmong. We looked to see if children in the classroom were represented in their classroom and school libraries. Were there books that talked about Vietnamese and Hmong families? We looked for the mirrors. Then we looked for the windows. In this PD, children of color needed to see themselves reflected in the literature, and White students needed to see beyond their world.

Mirrors and windows can be offered beyond books and media. Children talk with one another, watch the news, or listen to you engage with other adults. These are teaching opportunities. For example, when you have active shooter drills, fire drills, or dangerous weather drills, children are given an explanation. These drills are meant not to strike fear into children but to prepare them. In the same way, students can explore the legislative debate on firearms in our country and compare and contrast with legislation in other countries. We can help children understand the dialogue around global climate change, how the COVID-19 pandemic has ravaged low-income communities, and why we have food drives during the holidays. Along with the what, who, when, and where, our children deserve to know the why. The mirrors and windows we provide for our children allow them to make sense of their world.

A former graduate student of mine, a fifth-grade teacher, offers a great example of how to support sprouting and help students explore and learn from life outside the classroom. There was a controversy in another local school district about what was considered "banned hairstyles." All the hairstyles that were banned were styles that Black boys and girls would wear. As a Black teacher in a predominantly Black class, she and her students were offended by that district's rules. The teacher turned this display of overt injustice into a lesson. She used the English language arts standards to help students reflect on what the banned hairstyles meant for them, as children who wear the styles listed. The teacher facilitated the conversation so the students could talk about what was happening and came up with ideas to not internalize the school district's racist stance.

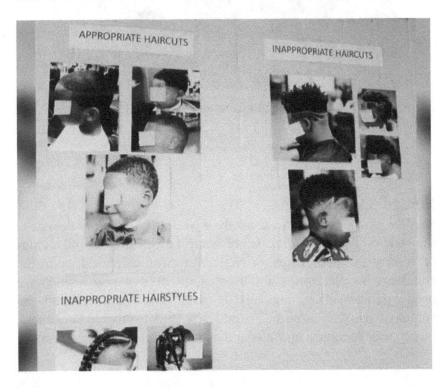

2019 · 👥

I believe the most important thing that I can teach students is how to advocate & think FOR THEMSELVES! We examined images of the "banned" hair cuts and styles today! Super excited about integrating art and writing into the discussion!

* * *

How to Sprout

Start by practicing with your family in your home. Boldly break the skewed and limited boundaries of WASP, European-centered tellings of history (United States or your European-colonized country). Humanize people, stories, and lived experiences of groups who have been traditionally marginalized and oppressed, viewed as complementary, or ignored to prioritize and legitimize Whiteness. Incorporate literature and media that act as mirrors and windows to a diversity of experiences. Remember to avoid reinforcing negative stereotypes and single-story narratives. Explore current events to help children understand multiple perspectives, feed their curiosity, sharpen their research skills, and actively participate in society.

Then expand to your friend group. Commit to intentional growth. Identify your local, immediate needs. Our needs were to overcome the casualties of color silencing and shaming, normalize diversity within our common humanity through media and field trips, equip ourselves and our children with a framework to understand our racialized society, and incorporate healthy language to form belonging perspectives. You can do this, too. The influence of your friend group will hopefully extend into your schools, where more parents and teachers can be invited to participate.

Identify like-minded peers, coworkers, and friends who are willing to commit to a learning journey as well. So that no one in the group feels the pressure of being the expert, look to well-designed educational resources like courses, teaching videos, expert-led workshops, and events. Choose well-designed, learning-centered opportunities over the common but less helpful discussion-centered gatherings. Such plenary-type events focus on story and opinion sharing only and usually don't offer the guided instruction or developmental process necessary to sustain growth. While making space to hear and share personal stories is significant, *human interest stories*, as we call them, cannot serve as your only source of education. Engaging in cross-racial conversations to *solve race/ism* can be helpful, but attempting to do so void of understanding race as a mechanism is emotionally taxing. Personal stories expressed by individuals or news headlines invoke an emotional response but often offer no historical context and can feed into anecdotal misunderstandings. Feeling pain over injustice is good. However, simply being angry or sorry does not sustain growth or change anything. We have left these types of sessions feeling depleted and discouraged.

As parents and teachers, we know that learning is a holistic process of acquiring new knowledge, skills, understanding, values, attitudes, behaviors, and preferences. And becoming antiracists to cultivate justice and belonging requires us to gain (1) new knowledge and understanding regarding our racialized context and (2) critical thinking skills for analyzing structural injustice, inequity, and unconscious biases. Developmentally designed learning experiences help you build the skills to reach your goals. Pedagogy matters. You wouldn't invite pre-schoolers to engage in calculus. Nor would you send them to a "courageous, community conversation on calculus" event in hopes that they'd master it. In the same way that pedagogy matters in how we teach and learn math, it matters to the same degree, if not more, for supporting our antiracism learning journey. Invest in pedagogically sound educational experiences that support growth and development.

For teachers and administrators, consider the changes that need to occur in your classroom and school policies and practices. Review your staff, student, and parent handbooks. Look for biases that may exist in these documents. Consider who might be privileged and who might be harmed by the policies in place within the school community. Explore school access. Many schools and teachers say they want parent involvement but have predetermined what that involvement looks like or assume that it will look the same for all parents. For example, some families do not have the luxury of attending a school performance, meeting, or teacher conference in the middle of the day. Expectations can be broadened so that parents can connect and contribute in various ways to performances by sewing costumes, building sets, and providing snacks and evening options for meetings and teacher conferences. All parents want what is best for their children. Increasing access to account for varying parent needs is vital.

Reflection and Practice
Reflection

1. Notice how cultivating justice and belonging in our homes overflowed into our other spheres of influence—neighbors, friends, schools, classrooms. This shifting culture approach requires a different way of thinking and being. What insight did you gain from our stories? What is something that we did that you could put into practice?
2. With whom and in what places can you support growth for adults and children?
3. How do your home values or curriculum give your students and children agency to see an issue and act?

4. In what ways are your classroom or school policies inclusive to family's diverse needs? Where do you see a need for improvement?

PRACTICE

1. Review the rubric in the Appendix. Look at your home or classroom library. First, do you know the specific racial, ethnic, and cultural background of your students or your child's classmates? Second, are the book authors in your home, classroom, or school library from various racial, ethnic, and cultural backgrounds? Are there stories that feature BIPOC protagonists? Are the protagonists diverse in their intersections of identity? Sit down with books in your library and follow the rubric. Note who is present and who is absent within your collection. Create a plan to integrate books that are more reflective of a diverse community.

2. Teachers, look at your curricula. What modern-day issues, like banned hairstyles, can be included in your planning and instruction? What is going on in the world of your students that may need to show up in the classroom?

3. As you sprout, consider ways to invite people in your sphere of influence to glean from your experience. Create or join a growth group.

CHAPTER 6
BUD: See and Celebrate Growth

*A flower is not better when it blooms than when it is merely a bud;
at each stage it is the same thing—a flower in the process of
expressing its potential.*

—Paulo Coelho, Lyricist and Novelist

Plant buds are an early indicator of new potential. A part of the blooming process, the bud is a small protuberance on the stem that develops into a flower, leaf, or shoot. Before they eventually swell, burst forth, and become new plant material, buds are tiny affirmations of all the growth that has previously occurred. The bud exemplifies endurance and is a tiny picture of intentional, consistent growth. While simple and small, buds expand in complexity, breadth, and beauty. We must acknowledge and express gratitude for the bud. Likewise, as we remain committed and consistent, we must remember to appreciate the growth that has occurred. Showing gratitude for small growth prepares us for more growth.

In Chapter 4, we acknowledged the need to grieve racism. In this chapter, we want you to learn to acknowledge and celebrate growth. Too often, people miss out on partaking in the joy of growth. During one of our *What LIES Between Us—Fostering First Steps Toward Racial Healing* online classes, a learner shared how she was discouraged by the social unrest around her. She appeared noticeably defeated as she shook her head and slumped toward the camera. We paused and honored her feelings. We certainly understand. But at the end of the live Zoom session, we encouraged her to look at how many people had chosen to give up weeks of their time to launch an antiracism learning journey. Daily, we get to support the growth of parents, students, teachers, administrators, and church and corporate leaders who are invested in uprooting scarcity ideology (i.e., steal, kill, and destroy to survive) and planting seeds to harvest justice and belonging. The growth cycle is arduous and slow. And if we don't acknowledge and appreciate our bud, we will give up on the process of becoming a flower.

Lucretia

I emerged from the auditorium of women anxious to reach the sun-drenched parking lot. I'd sat among a familiar sisterhood focused on connecting with one another while absorbing the speaker's encouraging words. However, my introvert self was ready to escape the crowd to find refuge in the solitude of the sun and to breathe in fresh warm air. That's when a smiling stranger, a White woman, approached me with a compliment and a proposition. She told me how much she loved Brownicity and the work I was doing. Then she invited me to connect with the director of her children's school because she believed my work would be a great asset. I was outwardly cordial. But in my mind, I rolled my eyes.

The *ask* was sincere. But this was in spring 2017. At that time, previous invitations to support teachers and teacher leaders in predominantly White formal learning spaces turned out to be veiled attempts to simply check the "diversity training" box. Most were not actually ready for the necessary investment, effort, and commitment. In one instance, a school with a predominantly White student population and an all-White teaching staff scheduled an hour-long workshop for me to teach staff how to engage with students regarding skin tone, ethnicity, and race. For context, this happened in 2016, just before the school year began and in the heat of the Trump–Clinton presidential campaign season. The teachers were present, but no one from the school's administration attended. Almost half the teachers knew me and leaned in with ease. However, a significant number of teachers were new to the school and met me with distrust. The distrusting group sat with terse looks and arms crossed, a clear sign of resistance.

When I shared the benefits of replacing race-blind or colorblind ideology with "conscious and informed language," one teacher asked, "Why should this matter to us at *this* school?" He was implying that because the school enrolled only a few students who are not White, the school staff need not concern themselves with the racialized realities of the outside world. I speculated that this teacher had absolved White students of all normal social development. Perhaps he thought that White children are not racialized and do not observe and wonder about phenotypic differences, their brains are not negotiating meaning around racial identity and social class, and they want no agency or responsibility in creating fairness. Perhaps this teacher believed that predominantly White spaces are incapable of producing racial or social injury.

I shared that when students have language and permission to acknowledge and call out overt racism, they are empowered to help enact change, to which a different teacher replied, "I don't want to teach my son to be an ally because then he might grow up to shoot police officers!" Needless to say, I was dumbfounded. I was appalled by their emboldened resistance to learn. I'd been invited to facilitate their growth, but many of the teachers were not ready or willing. Because she had anticipated that I would need her support, Michelle, a Black mom whose children attended the school, asked to serve as my workshop assistant. When the teacher made the ludicrous remark equating racial competence with shooting police officers, Michelle paused the workshop. She strategically disrupted the tension. She informed them that my father used to be a police officer, quelling their fears that my beginner-level workshop was a cloaked antipolice scheme. One of the teachers, Ms. Katherine, excited about my presentation, spoke up. She shared how ready and excited she was to have a framework, language, and competence to participate in creating a just and belonging classroom and school.

Now more than ever, we have access to great resources and research supporting the urgency for antiracism. However, in many cases, hearts and minds have not been cultivated to produce good growth. In this instance, the school leaders and teaching staff did not have a shared vision and goals. The leaders of the school did not attend the workshop. Without alignment and participation, collective growth is impossible, which enables fractures in the learning community.

As for the stranger who complimented my work and then invited me to her charter school, I reluctantly reached out to the director of her children's school. I presumed that the school director would ask me to do a 1-hour workshop with the school staff like the previous leader or perhaps maybe even do a 6-hour day of professional development. Based on my past experience, I was ready to reject her offer. The previous experience was too painful and disappointing. I was tired of seeing too little effort extended toward an endeavor that requires a lifetime of commitment. However, Ms. Jill, this school's director, was the first school leader I encountered who presented a long-term vision. As I listened to her proposal, I welled up with tears. I felt relieved for the school's children, family, and community. The director told me, "I'm not looking for someone to come to the school, drop a bomb, and then leave us to clean up the pieces." As you can imagine, I was relieved.

Ms. Jill proposed starting with a 5-year plan. Note that she understood a healthy onboarding process could take years. She envisioned a collective educational journey for the entire staff—teachers and administrators. She asked me if I would also be willing to serve as a consultant for the kindergarten through fifth grade teaching teams, the middle school and high school humanities teachers, and any teacher who wanted additional support. She wanted to know if I could be a guest reader for the early elementary classrooms and a guest speaker for the upper grade classes. Because teachers rely on support from parents, Ms. Jill proposed that we offer courses for parents as well. Finally, she asked me if I would be willing to design an elective course for the high school students. In my opinion, Ms. Jill laid out the ideal plan for a community schoolwide cultural elevation. I was ecstatic.

Before I began working with the staff, they had already set an intention to grow their understanding around the impact of social injustice in their community and school. They began as a small group asking questions and postured to learn. Then the small group expanded to a large group of staff members who organized a book study around Beverly Tatum's (1997/2017) *Why Are All the Black Kids Sitting Together in the Cafeteria?* They incorporated a group discussion guide and met regularly to walk through the book. We have included a sample of their book study guide in the Appendix.

Tatum's book offers a solid start for the very reason she wrote it. A clinical psychologist, Tatum designed *The Psychology of Racism*, a curriculum taught at various institutions. Following years of teaching, speaking, and publishing, Tatum noticed that her presentations were heavily attended by parents, educators, and community leaders. She wrote *Why Are All the Black Kids Sitting Together in the Cafeteria?: And Other Conversations About Race* for them. Through her research and background in education, she addresses our reluctance to talk with children about racism for fear that we will make otherwise race-blind children into racists. Tatum introduces her reader to the operational definition of racism and offers a framework for acknowledging and understanding racial identity development and dynamics in racial groups.

When I joined the school's staff the following year, the primary goal was to guide and support my colleagues. The monthly staff meetings were reserved for professional development where I, along with the Brownicity Team, taught *Foundations*, our onboarding curriculum designed to help beginners gain an analytical framework for examining race/ism in the United States. Over the course of several months, staff members were equipped with a historical, political, and social context for understanding how systemic and structural racism is sustained.

Even in the best of circumstances where every single person has agreed to collectively cultivate just and belonging learning spaces, we know each of us may be at a different starting point. Some of us have a nuanced and complex understanding of how racism has shaped institutional structures. Others of us recognize interpersonal overt racism only when one person invokes trauma on another. And when considering how to confront racism, primarily our thinking is limited to bad behavior—for example, addressing how children behave in school. But we often fail to consider how school is a tool of systemic racism and furthermore how it can be used to deconstruct racism.

How We Started with the Staff

To gage the overall comfort level around talking about race/ism, we asked the staff to complete prelaunch questions:

1. Are you comfortable talking about skin tone and race/ism?
2. What prompts your thoughts or discussions about race/ism?
3. As a child, did you discuss race/ism with adults at home or in school?
4. Do you feel it is appropriate to discuss race/ism with children and students?
5. If you talk about race/ism, what has helped you discuss race/ism with children and students? What resources do you use?
6. How many years of teaching experience do you have?

Data results revealed that the staff's experiences varied. There were teachers who did not feel comfortable discussing race (20 percent) and did not discuss race in their own home (40 percent). Meanwhile, others were comfortable (80 percent) and discussed race at home (40 percent). We also recognized that teachers were more comfortable teaching and talking about racism in conjunction with civil rights leaders and famous Americans. They, however, were less efficacious regarding critical analyses of the larger systemic influences like those that caused the Civil Rights Movement.

Regardless of prior antiracism education and engagement, we wanted everyone to have a mutual understanding of contributing factors to current racial injustice. We wanted everyone to gain a shared understanding of problematic practices to engage in shared problem-solving. The monthly staff meetings were designated as our classroom. The meeting agenda for 7 months of the school year was the same: Foundations with Dr. Berry. Lessons were designed to help the staff build a sound knowledge base and develop perspectives beyond popular discourse and uninformed opinions. Units included:

What Is Race?

What Is Race/ism?

What Are the Costs of Race/ism?

Race/ism and Immigration

Analysis of Power, Politics, and Privilege

Brain and Belief Bias: Narratives, Representations, Stereotypes, Media Literacy

Staff were assigned heart work (i.e., homework) to complete between monthly meetings. Heart work included reflective prompts to support introspection, critical thinking, application, and imagination. Because racial competency has not been normalized, most of us do not know how to critically think about institutionalized racial injustice beyond American chattel slavery and racist incidents shared in the news. Reflective prompts for journaling help us become aware of how we've been formed and informed by racial messaging—in other words, how we've been racialized. Answering the prompts supported an examination of our own mental and emotional processes. Journaling allows us to put our thoughts on paper, look at them, and see where we need the most support.

With a practical understanding of contributing ideologies (e.g., colorblindness and White supremacy) and interpersonal and systemic dynamics (e.g., unconscious bias and privilege), each staff member could have a broadened awareness of self, "others," and our interconnected society. Early in the process, a few teachers anticipated that they would be told what and how to teach differently. But ultimately, we did not want to dictate teaching protocols. We did not want to offer a diversity, equity, and inclusion checklist—another tactical box to climb into. Our goal was to lay a foundation—to spark agency, courage, and creativity in staff. That way, if they chose to be transformative leaders in their classrooms and school, they would have the fortitude, autonomy, and authority to do so.

One of the middle school teachers had this to say about the Foundations course:

> To say I learned is really an understatement. My understanding has been changed—and my actions and statements have been forever altered. I entered the class thinking I already knew so much about race, racism, and bias in the United States. I did know plenty, but I quickly learned that for a variety of reasons, my understanding was quite limited.

I honestly think I could take the Foundations course again and again and increase my understanding each time as I work to not only understand the systematic nature of racism historically, politically, and socially but also grow as an antiracist teacher and member of this society.

I was relieved to see teachers grappling with the content and challenging their held beliefs and practices. I was honored to witness their willingness to learn. Even though a few staff members did not agree with some of the information presented in the Foundations curriculum, they attended the sessions and participated. Meanwhile, when one group completed the Tatum Book Study, another small group began. I was invited to participate in one of the small groups.

I was also invited to join grade-level teacher planning meetings. During these meetings, teachers worked with each other to plan lessons. They invited me to weigh in on thoughts and questions about content that fostered a just and belonging curriculum. For example, during the kindergarten teacher planning meeting, a teacher asked me to review a few children's books that talked about race and skin tone. Another simply needed me to be a sounding board for a lesson she wanted to develop on Indigenous Americans. And a fifth-grade team invited me to their planning meeting to act as an accountability partner to perceive potential blind spots.

How We Started with the Students
ELEMENTARY

That year, I was invited to visit each grade of the elementary school. For most of the kindergarten through fourth-grade classes, I visited as a guest reader and led a funshop with the students. The purpose of the funshop is to help children build community, connection, and positive pathways regarding diversity within humanity, offer developmentally appropriate language and a framework, provide informed definitions of common terms, and give context and permission to learn and talk about phenotypic, cultural, ethnic, and racial distinctions without the stigma or fear attached to talking about race/ism, while also building empathy, respect, and understanding. If anyone needs more proof that children see skin color and notice differences, this funshop offers affirmation. To give children language and understanding, I read *All the Colors We Are—The Story of How We Get Our Skin Color* by Katie Kissinger (2014) and *The Colors of Us* by Karen Katz (1999). Immediately afterward, the children pour out questions and comments. It's as if being given permission to talk about their observations released the floodgates of inquiry and curiosity. Each time I did the funshop, it yielded the same result: the children had significantly more questions than we adults had time to answer.

If melanin is brown, why is my hair red?

Can people with more melanin jump higher than people with less melanin?

Why is some hair straight and some hair curly?

Why does your hair go up instead of down?

If melanin is brown, why am I called White?

Also during the workshops, we were able to intercept negative messaging. For example, during the workshop, a Black student shared that he did not like his skin because an older White student told him his skin was dirty. And an Indian child had internalized that she should lighten her skin. Because the children were given language and space to share, we adults were able to intercept negative messaging that may have remained internalized.

It was a need and my joy to affirm every student. However, I felt it was my responsibility to relieve students of color from the burden of educating their White peers about differences in skin tone and hair texture. When a student appears to be in the racial minority in the classroom or group, they often become the object of their peers' inquiries about differences, which can make them feel othered. Children are naturally curious and should be able to explore within safe boundaries. However, teachers, parents, and caregivers should not evade the responsibility and opportunity to educate children about something as basic and common as phenotype. Every child needs to know they belong.

These funshops inspired me to create *Hues of You—An Activity Book for Learning About the Skin You Are In* (2022) and along with

Tehia and others from the Brownicity Team, design the bKids course, *Let's Learn About.* The funshop, the activity book, and the *Let's Learn About* course support natural curiosity, spark exploration, and inspire engagement while normalizing the diversity in our common humanity. The activities and content help learners develop connections, understanding, respect, and empathy.

MIDDLE LEVEL AND HIGH SCHOOL

At the middle and high school level, I was invited to consult with teachers in content areas like English, leadership seminar, history, civics, and social studies. Teachers were free and encouraged to consult with me about how to talk about and address race in units and lessons. Or if they needed a particular historically hidden or excluded story, narrative, or perspective, I helped them find it. I was also invited into classrooms as a guest speaker. I listened to students discuss complicated topics. I brought living color to the unit on Jim Crow and the Civil Rights Movement. I shared about the time I spent in post-apartheid South African schools. And in a public speaking class, I was simply the cool guest who had done a TED Talk on how to talk about race with children.

When students unfortunately perpetuated interpersonal racist incidents, I was able to help staff think through how to address the issue through a restorative lens. For example, an instance was reported to staff that some White students, even though they were denied permission, were touching the hair of their Black classmates. As a result, Black students felt violated and disrespected in a space where they belong and should feel safe. While teachers and staff affirmed the Black student, I collated resources to help bring context and understanding to why touching a Black person's hair without permission is problematic and not justified by White curiosity. The resources were shared with staff and parents.

While macro culture will be reflected in school, our schools can be just and belonging learning environments that foster a more sophisticated and shared understanding of that macro culture. Such incidents like this can be used to educate and help all students. While students may come to school informed by harmful agendas, they can depart informed by care for common humanity. Students can be taught and expected to respect their classmates who experience the world differently than they do. Subsequently, students can have a positive impact on the culture outside of school.

That year, I also worked with the high school leadership seminar students to develop the high school elective What Is Race/ism? (now called Antiracism 101). I shared some of the Foundations course content with the upperclass-level students. They served as end users on our participatory design team and understood that they were making significant contributions to the school. They were asked:

1. If you were teaching this course, besides teaching the history of racist policies and practices, what other elements and topics would you include?
2. What do you think about addressing the following topics in the course?
   - Microaggressions
   - White privilege and White supremacy
   - The N-word
   - Antiracism
   - Political correctness
   - Immigration
3. What other topics would you include?
4. What contemporary issues or current events would you include?
5. Field trips. Are there any local places you'd like to visit that would contribute to enriching the course experience?
6. Guest speakers. Who are local leaders and speakers who might be willing to visit the class or have our class visit them?
7. Projects. What types of projects would you enjoy?
8. What should be the objectives of the course?
9. Do you have any other thoughts or recommendations? Please share.
10. What do you think about the proposed course title What Is Race/ism?
11. What do you think about the course description?

    The purpose of this course is to offer students an analytical framework for examining race/ism in the United States. Students will be equipped with a historical, political, and social context for understanding race/ism and how it is sustained. Course content will allow students to build a sound knowledge base and develop a perspective beyond popular discourse and uninformed opinions. With a practical understanding of contributing ideologies and interpersonal and systemic dynamics, students will have a broadened awareness of themselves, others, and our interconnected society. Assignments and projects will strengthen students to practice transformative leadership in their spheres of influence.

The high school leadership seminar students gave me important feedback and direction, which helped shape the elective that was offered the following year.

PARENTS

The staff were not alone in their efforts. Parents were able to participate as well. The school held advisory meetings for parents to learn more about and connect to and align with the vision. The series designed for parents was called Understanding Race/ism. Parents were sent this invitation:

Although race/ism is a complex and nuanced topic, it does not have to be scary and volatile. We've created a safe space to learn the difficult history of race/ism, engage in healthy conversations and ask and answer questions. Our goal is to GROW together so that we grow TOGETHER.

This five-week series will be facilitated by our own, Dr. Lucretia Carter Berry, mom of three [school] elementary students and founder of Brownicity—Many Hues, One Humanity. The series features media screenings, resources (online and live), skillfully guided group discussions, and facilitator-lead engagement.

Parents who enrolled and attended were taught the same foundational content as the staff. We hosted two 5-week courses for parents. One class was scheduled for five consecutive Sunday afternoons for parents who could not attend the other class which met during the school day. Both were held at the school. Giving parents the same instruction and support that the staff received contributed to cultivating a healthy root system—a culture shift. Mutually informed people seldom disagree. When parents and teachers have a shared vision and share in problem-solving, they manifest shared solutions.

I don't pretend to be a know-it-all. And I am not an endless source of expertise. When teachers, parents, and students asked questions I couldn't answer or they needed understanding that I could not articulate, I reached out to specialists in universities and local communities. Scholars and leaders in the community who are immersed in research and practice were more than happy to assist. Professors of education, sociology, social work, theology, and history either met directly with staff or consulted with them through email. Tangibly connecting the school to local universities and leaders helps cultivate community. On several occasions, I reached out to Tehia to answer questions and give direction. She then applied for and was awarded a research grant to support teachers as they continued to build their sense of efficacy in teaching antiracism-oriented content. We will discuss more of that project in subsequent chapters.

Seeing and Celebrating Growth

Over the course of one school year, growth occurred. We were budding. The following school year, I sent out a survey to collect observable and measurable progress. Teachers were asked:

1. Was addressing race/ism as a system instead of just individual bigoted behavior new to you?
2. Does understanding the ages at which children begin observing phenotypic differences and mimicking society impact your teaching practice?
3. Do you feel prepared to talk about skin tone or race/ism with students? Colleagues? Parents?
4. Have there been opportunities to discuss skin tone or race/ism in your classroom?
5. If there have been opportunities to discuss skin tone or race/ism in your classroom, who initiated it—you, student, administrator, or parent?

For the teachers who completed the survey, half said that understanding race/ism as a system instead of just individual bigoted behavior was new to them. A total of 83 percent reported that gaining an understanding that children are not colorblind and have questions about race impacted their teaching practice. After our year of budding, teachers felt prepared to talk with students and colleagues about skin tone, race, and racism. Half did not feel prepared to talk with parents about this topic.

And 84 percent of teachers reported that in their classrooms there were opportunities to discuss skin tone or race/ism. When asked who initiates the conversations about race, 47 percent of the teachers said they initiated the discussion, 10 percent reported that administrators or staff initiated the discussion, and 10 percent reported that parents initiated the discussion. The largest group to initiate a discussion or conversation about skin tone, race, and racism were students—57 percent.

Teachers, administrators, and parents are busy teaching, leading, and parenting. Therefore, making time to acknowledge and chart growth—especially incremental growth—may not be a priority. But if we fail to see and celebrate the incremental growth, we will feel like we are always striving toward antiracism, justice, and belonging but never getting anywhere. So I did my best to record and collect stories and testimonials. I documented the stories teachers and parents told me and noted my own observations. I also sent this request to the staff:

> Hi wonderful people!
> Were you motivated to do something differently (anything, could even be how you think) as a result of something you learned or something that happened along our [school initiative], understanding race/ism journey?

Here is some of what was captured and celebrated.

After parents completed the Foundations course, three of them organized an on-going gathering to continue to foster community and understanding. One of the outings included a group viewing of the movie *The Hate You Give* (2018) followed by a debrief.

At least two school families were able to get their churches to go through the faith-based version of the *Foundations* course called *What LIES Between Us - Fostering First Steps Toward Racial Healing*.

The following school year, What Is Race/ism? was listed as an elective. The course also featured a What Is Race/ism? library offering books and resources by antiracism scholars and authors. The students who enrolled in the course shared what they were learning with their peers and parents. As a result of more intentional dialogue, some students initiated school clubs to support learning, understanding, and each other. One of the teachers in Tehia's research study became the advisor for that club. The teacher served as an intermediary between the students and the administrative team and helped students to advocate for themselves.

As they planned lessons for the following year, teachers invited guest artists from culturally diverse backgrounds. Teachers also requested more curriculum resources and literature by authors and creatives of color. Attention was given to everyday items like crayons, Band-Aids, and dolls to represent various skin tones.

The Tatum Book Study small groups continued to meet.

An African American teacher said that she felt she could have more intentional engagement with students and staff—especially when she needed to address something race related.

After teaching units on Dr. Martin Luther King, Jr. as a boy, Dorothy Counts, and Ruby Bridges, a kindergarten teacher observed her students comparing their skin tones and making connections to the people and history they had just learned about. Her students were open and informed, not ashamed or embarrassed.

Another kindergarten teacher shared about how each of her students named their skin tones beautiful hues of brown.

Double vanilla, horchata, medium dark sunshine, pasta noodles, White chocolate, spaghetti noodles, peach ice cream, tan, vanilla donut, whipped cream, peaches, noodles with pepper on top, vanilla nut, vanilla Tic Tacs, unicorn, sand, almond, light wood, chocolate chip cookie, and toast

In a predominantly White classroom, these students have the capacity and permission to openly talk about and respect phenotypic differences.

A teacher shared her sentiment about the year-long learning journey:

> You have made me feel comfortable to let kids just talk. I don't feel as though I have to steer their conversation in a different direction simply because I am uncomfortable talking about certain topics or issues. You have empowered me and given me confidence to open the door to talk about issues regarding women's rights, the Great Migration, Jim Crow laws in the South. . . . I have introduced new artists such as Jacob Lawrence, Richard Lewis, and Jean-Michel Basquiat. I revamped art lessons for Faith Ringgold to show how she tells the stories of what and who are important in her life through story quilts. I am encouraging children to make art about journeys in American history which historically are not taught, like the Great Migration. These stories are being researched currently by second graders. You have raised my awareness for all students. I can allow them to explore and talk without me having a bias about what is important for them. Today a boy was shocked when he learned that we have never had a female president. I just let him talk about it. Another student told her group that "White people used to have water fountains and Black people had their own, but they called it 'colored,' and that wasn't very nice." And when her group asked why it wasn't nice, she said that her mom told her this, and her mom is Black, too, and that it was the same water—not White or colored water.

This teacher then expressed her appreciation for the learning journey, one that was intentional, consistent, and respectful—one that was cultivated for her to grow. Neither the garden nor the gardener was hostile. This teacher felt cared for. A teacher leader shared this about the yearlong experience:

> [Dr. Berry] specifically developed a curriculum that was not faith based to meet our needs as a public school. Our staff is forever changed. We are grateful to continue our work towards

dismantling racism as educators under her guidance. She supports our teachers with curriculum development and lesson planning. She has brought in experts from her Brownicity Team who have grown our staff, as well. She has offered parent education sessions that have deeply impacted families within our community. Parents have thanked us profusely for bringing such a wonderful educator in to help them understand this painful and complex topic. I have been told repeatedly by parents that this education under her leadership has equipped them to have important conversations with their children.

In short, Dr. Berry brings a plethora of resources to help grow our community. We are grateful for the work she does. We as educators have an integral responsibility in helping to dismantle racism and it begins with making sure we all learn the history we were never taught.

We then created an online version of the Foundations course so that teachers who joined the staff (after our initial year of ground work) could have access to the onboarding content. New staff members were asked to take the course so that they could have a mutual understanding of the vision and direction.

Tehia

After I had my own children, I was positioned on the parental side of school and schooling. I began to think about schools as a parent, not just as a teacher. This is when my eyes were truly opened. I had a beloved colleague who bragged about how his children were attending an awesome school. His kids loved being there. The teachers loved being there. Everyone loved being there. Because I didn't have children at the time, I didn't think much about it. It just sounded like a great school. When I was invited to help with professional development, I observed how teachers and caregivers showed up for *all* kids.

The more time I spent in the school conducting research via supporting teachers, the more I realized what a difference the administration made. They had a vision and philosophy for how adults and children should be treated. Ultimately, I concluded that the administration at this school supports teachers, families, and children in a way that should happen at every school.

How to Bud

Parents, teachers, and school leaders can share the vision, set a collective precedent, and establish direction. Think about where you want to be in 5–10 years. We shared in Chapter 2 that cultivating a just and belonging learning community must be embodied, not performed. Policies can be amended with a stroke of a pen (well, sort of), but tilling the collective soil of hearts and minds can take a while longer. Understanding the necessity of longevity will help you be proactive rather than reactive and give you space to cultivate and create communities, schools, and classrooms where all children know they belong.

Dr. Martin Luther King, Jr.'s 1967 speech addressed to members of the Southern Christian Leadership Conference was titled "Where Do We Go from Here: Chaos or Community?" The title sounds ripe for today, doesn't it? In the speech, Dr. King continues to advocate for human rights and a sense of hope. He first acknowledges the accomplishments of civil rights organizations and leaders. He then pressed the listeners to "recognize where we are now." And finally, he said:

The plant of freedom has grown only a bud and not yet a flower.

In 1967, after the Civil Rights Act was passed, at a time when many of our nation's citizens had pushed hard to manifest so much change, Dr. King reminded them that we are not even close to the finish line. Yes, a bud is significant. The presence of a bud means that the soil and seed are doing what they were designed to do—that a root structure is thriving. A bud is evidence of proper nourishment from the sun and rain. But a bud is not the flower or the fruit we are reaching for. A bud means that we have more growing to do.

Reflection and Practice

REFLECTION

1. What growth have you seen in your home, classroom, or school? What has taken root and begun to bud? What have beliefs and practices changed?
2. How do you acknowledge and record growth?
3. What do you need permission (from yourself) to do or try next?
4. What topic would you like to learn more about so that you can approach and teach it with confidence? Why? What about the topic or content concerns you?

PRACTICE

1. Revise or create a lesson through an antiracism lens. What do you need to understand to do this? How can the lesson include multiple perspectives? How can it affirm belonging?
2. Craft a classroom newsletter inviting parents to engage in your lesson with their children. Include books, documentaries, or podcasts to give them perspective. Here is an example:

    This unit on exploring historical and contemporary Native American contributions to North Carolina will allow us to investigate resources like:

    Indigenous People's History of the US, NCpedia.org, NC Museum of History, and *PBS.*

    We will use standards (ELA) RL.4.1 Refer to details and examples in a text when explaining what the text says explicitly and when drawing inferences from the text; (Music) 4.CR.1.1 Understand how music has affected, and is reflected in the culture, traditions, and history of North Carolina; (Digital Learning) 3a. Students plan and employ effective research strategies to locate information and other resources for their intellectual or creative pursuits; and Math NC.4.MD.4 Make a representation of data and interpret data in a frequency table, scaled bar graph, or line plot.

    Our final project, we invite you to learn with your child as we explore our North Carolina history.

CHAPTER 7
WEED: Uproot Growth Inhibitors

"Don't let the tall weeds cast a shadow on the beautiful flowers in your garden."

—Steve Maraboli, Speaker, Best-selling Author, and Behavioral Scientist

Weeding is a necessary part of gardening. Weeds can aggressively dislocate healthy plants, robbing them of the nutrients that they need. We want to ensure that helpful, healthy things bloom. We weed out the things that do not add value and prohibit healthy growth. Just as editors delete words that don't work or photographers crop out the distractions, we can uproot beliefs, practices, and policies that work against cultivating justice and belonging.

* * *

Susan, Latinx High School Teacher
In 1980, I arrived with my family of origin from Costa Rica. We lived with relatives in Long Island. Because we moved around a lot, we moved from school to school. We attended schools where often we were the first and only Spanish-speaking students. We were placed in classrooms based on our English proficiency or lack thereof. At one point, one of the schools hired a Spanish-speaking woman for us. She was like our personal angel.

I was tested and skipped a grade. Meanwhile, my brother and male cousins were removed from regular classes and placed in a special education class. Our parents were not happy about this, but they respected the school's decisions and didn't question it. On the other hand, I questioned everything, including why I was not allowed to read the same book as my classmate. I also had to consistently advocate for myself—from questioning why others had book choices and I did not to inquiring about why certain classes were selected for me versus choosing them for myself.

Meanwhile, I observed that my brother was stigmatized and labeled. The school determined that he was not going to excel. This really bothered me. Even as a child, I wondered why my brother and cousins were placed in a special education class. Afterall, we came from the same home and background. And my brother would even help me with my homework. I knew he was bright and fully capable of being in classes alongside me.

While I saw my brother and cousins being put on a pathway to prison, I learned to advocate for myself. Because I was in proximity to other students talking about college, I put myself on the path to college. While working in the guidance counselor's office, I asked how to prepare for college and was enrolled in Upward Bound, a college preparatory program. Through Upward Bound, I received help and support and saw people who looked like me go to college. When I saw other Latinos go to college, I knew I could. I can still recall at the young age of 12 how, at home, I constantly asked my mother if I was legally able to attend college. This is when she began the process for my siblings and me to start the green card process.

I believe that due to being placed on a special education track, my brother and cousins internalized that they were not good enough. Although my family discouraged them, my brother and cousins were encouraged by the school counselor to join the military. Eventually, they served time in prison and therefore were never allowed to become U.S. citizens.

My family believed that my brother would get his citizenship. But after prison, my brother was deported immediately. As soon as his sentence was done, Immigration and Naturalization Service (INS) officers rearrested him and deported him. In fact, in the courtroom, after being given his release, immigration immediately came in and took him away. My brother, who could no longer speak Spanish, was sent back to Costa Rica, where he had not lived since he was a small child.

Now, as a teacher, I wonder how no one in the school saw my brother and cousins for their value. Not a single professional educator expected them to do well. Instead, my brother and cousins were treated like failures. It's heartbreaking to think how the school system purposely and intentionally failed them.

* * *

Based on our experiences, we believe that any great garden *will* have weeds. Along your growth journey, you will not get things right all the time. There will be mishaps. You will make mistakes. There will be conflict that you have to confront. But remember that a setback can be a setup for a comeback. You can learn from the experience and keep growing. We hope that what we share here will help you identify potential weeds and offer insight for pruning.

Extraction

Ideally, you will get to work alongside and glean from people who have professional or lived experience with antiracism. Please remember to recognize, honor, and compensate your colaborers for their time, innovation, and resources. If we had $100 for each time a well-meaning parent, teacher, leader, or institution has asked us to give generously of our time, attention, and expertise without compensation or citation, we would be millionaires. We, separately, have been invited to "brainstorming" meetings with well-resourced people and organizations who want to learn more about what we are doing—not to collaborate with us or fund our innovation but to extract our ideas and recreate what we are doing for themselves. Extraction is injustice.

I (Lucretia) personally have been invited to meet with leaders who expressed an appreciation for my work. One educational institution wanted to employ me to teach a core subject but use my antiracism education expertise to help a group of White men create an antiracism program. They were not planning to pay me for my contribution to their antiracism education program. A few other leaders of well-resourced organizations, after meeting with me, used my course model to create courses of their own. These leaders were recognized, honored, and paid well for what they "created." Years ago, I designed an arts program for youth and presented the proposal to a few local churches who had youth groups. One youth pastor was really excited about my idea. Enthusiastically, he said, "I'll get back to you." He did not. Some time later when I visited the church for an event, I saw that he had removed my image from the art program description, added his own, and implemented the program. My/his flier hung on the church bulletin board. Recently, a leader of an organization asked for my insight via private message. She then copied and pasted my lengthy, well thought out, carefully crafted personal response into a public post to her mass of followers as her own statement. I was shocked and disappointed.

We surmise that because the United States has such a long history of extracting from Black women—chattel slavery, mammying, science experiments, rape, maids, minimum pay—perhaps it feels normal to take from us without giving anything in return. Stop stealing. Stop expecting something for nothing. Instead of extraction, try appreciation, compensation, and collaboration. As an antiracist, you get to disrupt the violent practices inherited through structural racism. Because you cannot do this work in isolation, think about how you will appreciate and honor your colaborers when you

- Change your behavior because you are inspired by another parent.
- Implement a great new lesson due to the time you've spent working with a teaching team member.
- Schedule a chat or time with someone to get their take on something.
- Use a colaborer's product as a starting point to create your own product.
- Are able to create and grow an initiative due to working with someone who has been at this for a long time.

You are benefiting from their emotional labor, education, professional experience, creativity, courage, innovation, and skill.

Think about how to give back. Too often, White people get funded, supported, paid, published, acknowledged, celebrated, and rewarded for less or the same antiracism efforts for which BIPOC have been ignored or divested. Each time this happens, monies that should be reinvested in BIPOC creatives are instead allocated to people, companies, organizations, and spaces who have no roots in antiracism. As we collaborate, let's normalize paying, citing, supporting, and honoring those who are helping us grow. Push and pull your colaborers up instead of stepping on their necks for leverage.

Perfection

You don't have to be perfect or an expert. Give yourself grace to be human. Expect to mess up. Let go of the pressure and stress of perfectionism, and accept the fact that you will not always get it right. Consider that at times you might say the wrong words, miss the mark on a response, have well-planned lessons or conversations fall flat, or have students accuse you of not being fair. Because you've built trusting relationships with families, students, and coworkers, the mistakes you make are viewed in the context of the community's collective learning journey. When the whole community of parents, teachers, and leaders are learning together, no one within the community gets ostracized for making a mistake. Additionally, when your community (parents, leaders, teachers) contributes to your curriculum and practices, those little hiccups are less detrimental.

Isolation

A White teacher reached out to us to get our advice about a very important and necessary piece of content. In the reenactment of a historical document, the narrator reads aloud the N-word. She wanted to discuss and explore the risk versus the rewards of including the audio from a pedagogical and critical perspective. Together, we went back and forth listing pros and cons for which approach to take, the prework for contextualizing the audio, and how the audio might impact the few Black students in a classroom where most of their peers are White. We gave her space to make her own decision based on student and class readiness.

We also talked about the importance of teaching White students to not turn and stare at Black students during lessons about America's subjugation of Black people and chattel slavery. Students of color have asked us why White students peer over at them when the lesson is about someone of color. The teacher recognized this behavior. She then noted how when lessons are about White suffragettes, the class does not turn and stare at the White girls.

This was the teacher's response to having access to support:

Thank you both so much for your insight. You have given me a great jumping off point and have added perspectives in your responses that I wouldn't have thought of. I've looked into an intergenerational trauma TED Talk that I think, moving forward, would help my students to understand the concept.

Lucretia, I agree that reminding students that [staring] at anyone belonging to any group that they don't identify as their own, isn't deemed polite or appropriate. We talked yesterday about a way to address this issue. I think I'll approach it from the standpoint of, because this is OUR collective history of the United States (as you pointed out in your earlier email, Lucretia), let's make sure we are reflecting on how we as individuals are processing this. Not as someone on the outside of the directly mentioned group but rather, how OUR history is affecting all of us. Staring seems to suggest that students are processing this history as "that's THEIR history" when really, we should make the shift to "this group was directly affected during X-time period, AND we all need to process how this continues to affect ALL OF US today, including the group originally targeted.

Again, I really appreciate both of you taking time out to look over the video, give suggestions, and continue to help me navigate through this.

You don't have to have all the answers or figure things out in isolation. Remember to collaborate with and glean insight from other teachers, parents, and leaders. Don't let your ego get in the way of asking questions and asking for help. You deserve to have support.

Denying the Dignity of Others

Content is important. But people are more important. At the beginning of the school year, instead of introducing new content, we recommend implementing a unit zero. Inspired by *Culturally Responsive Teaching and the Brain—Promoting Authentic Engagement and Rigor Among Culturally and Linguistically Diverse Students* (2015) by Zaretta L. Hammond, a unit zero allows you to dedicate the first 2 weeks of school to building community with your students and families. This is a time to lay a foundation and nurture your classroom culture. For early elementary teachers, the first 2 weeks of school is a great time to incorporate *Hues of You—An Activity Book for Learning About the Skin You Are In* (2022) by Lucretia Berry. Also, we designed the Brownicity bKids course *Let's Learn About* to give learners a healthy, belonging language and a framework for building empathy, respect, understanding, and connection. Your students can get to know you, and you can get to know your students. You get to see them in their full humanity, and they get to see you in your full humanity. Each of you gets to bring your whole self to the classroom.

On one occasion, we were asked to help plan a day-long interactive exhibition for middle school students. The living exhibit was inspired by *RACE: Are We So Different?*, a project of the American Anthropological Association and funded by the Ford Foundation and National Science Foundation. The middle school event was designed to address the topics of race from three different perspectives—history, science, and everyday experience—to tell a dynamic story with a deep social impact. On the day that we were training teachers to lead the various activities and presentations, we sensed that a teacher either was not ready to lead or did not appreciate the content. So, we paused the project.

The teachers who were excited about the exhibit and ready to lead were disappointed. But we knew it would not be wise to bring students into a learning experience that teachers were not ready for. Later, we met with the teacher who was uncomfortable with the content. Among other things, she did not believe that middle school children should be learning about race as a construct and structural racism. Although the project featured resources from the American Anthropological Association, the teacher believed that the resources were politically progressive. Gaining clarity about her reluctance helped us see potential walls and stumbling blocks for people with a similar background and political affiliation. Pausing to hear her perspective helped us better prepare for future participants.

In a different setting, I (Tehia) had to leave a group that I loved because the White women coleaders were toxic to the Black women who were also in leadership. I was talked over and interrupted. I was subjected to passive-aggressive comments. Though I was the lead on the design, if my work did not meet their expectations, I was discredited. The most frustrating part of this experience was that because they are White women with social and political capital, I felt like I couldn't be honest with them without fear of retribution.

As we dismantle brutal systems, we need to be gentle with people. We must truly see each other—as humans who have been shaped and formed by the very thing we are disrupting and breaking apart. But we must not break people. We must hear the biography over the ideology. Otherwise, we might cause more trauma and injury. Systems have been careless, and we want to do better. We have to be caring.

Fear of Discomfort

"What if being called a racist, or doing something racist is the start of the conversation, and not the end of it?" I (Tehia), was at American University's Summer Institute on Education Equity and Justice conference when professorial lecturer Traci Dennis asked this, and a light bulb went off in my head. That simple sentence articulated what I'd been doing all the while. How can we help folks turn toward rather than turn away after hearing the word race or antiracism? We cannot be afraid of being "called in" as Smith College professor Loretta Ross describes in her 2020 *New York Times* piece. If someone offends, "calling in" allows for attention or correction in a private way so there is opportunity for the offender to learn what they did and how they caused harm, versus "calling out," which is more of the public shaming of someone for the harm they may have caused. Calling in is contextual—someone you are in community with, or your discernment tells you the harm was unintentional can be called in. On the other hand, people who intend to harm may not get access to being called in. They may need public correction or an immediate conclusion to the conversation.

Lack of Fortitude

Intentionally misleading efforts to weaponize and spread disinformation about critical race theory (CRT) have nurtured a resistance to teaching and learning for justice and belonging. This age-old political strategy of fearmongering and spreading confusion to garner partisan allegiance unfortunately invades our homes, classrooms, communities, and worst of all our psyches. This strategy is not new; it's simply rebranded—recall resistance to school desegregation. While this type of resistance is a pain, you can use it to establish boundaries and a protocol for how to engage when the confusion attempts to cast a shadow on your lovely garden.

On several occasions, we have been asked to help quell CRT dumpster fires in families, communities, churches, schools, and minds. But if we commit all our resources to putting out fires, who will cultivate the garden? We would rather use the water to nourish growth than extinguish every fire launched by political pyromaniacs! With each request to address fears invoked by politicized bureaucracy, we ask ourselves: Is this an educational opportunity? Will this help teachers and parents? Or will this drain our resources and waste our time?

Leaders should consistently share a schoolwide vision for justice and belonging. Clarity is kind. Administrators and teachers must institute protocol for engaging with parents and community members who lack clarity regarding your direction and intention. Because conflict is stressful, having a plan in place will help navigate the rough terrain. For example, if a parent is concerned or worried about school and classroom practices, who do they address first, an administrator or a teacher? How are parental concerns documented and filed? Does your plan to resolve conflict include a pathway for maintaining trust between parents and the school? How will you care for traumatized teachers and students? How will you make sure that each person involved is seen, valued, and heard?

Lack of Self-Care

Parenting brings us joy. Teaching brings us joy. Both require so much of us. As parents and teachers, we are the constant, consistent caregivers—giving care to our families and giving care to our communities and schools. However, we rarely give care to ourselves. The old saying goes, "You can't pour from an empty cup." We have to prioritize care for ourselves—not just so that we can continue to consistently take care of others but also because we need and deserve care!

Many of us who are choosing to cultivate justice and belonging are being met with resistance from forces fueled by political propagandists. We won't give attention, time, and space to the resistance here, as we have dedicated these pages to supporting and encouraging you. However, we must acknowledge that the trauma from the drama is devastating and at times debilitating. When someone uses social media to spew misinformation about us or our work, it hurts. And as parents, teachers, and leaders, we cannot bring the trauma into our homes, classrooms, or schools. We cannot internalize it or allow it to shape and inform how we parent and teach. If we don't make space for our wounds to heal, they will fester. We don't want to bleed all over our children and students.

Kimberly Owen, MA LCMHC, EMDR, therapist and founder of Sage Healing and Wellness, talked to our facilitator cohort about how people working on the front lines of dismantling systemic racism and unraveling social injustice experience exhaustion:

> Social injustice fatigue can alter the body in many ways to the point of affecting sleep, foggy thinking, and emotional dysregulation. This can affect your whole being—mind, body and spirit. The danger in this is that people resort to coping mechanisms that don't serve them well. Maladaptive coping mechanisms are compartmentalization, impulsivity. . ., along with overwhelming emotions that lead to deregulation. . . Some people just shut down and freeze while the amygdala goes into high gear.
>
> —Kimberly Owen, MA LCMHC, EMDR, therapist and founder of Sage Healing and Wellness

She advises that we prioritize self. Healing and recovery are essential to justice and belonging.

Punishing Ideological Differences

Learning about the unjust, exclusionary policies and practices we've inherited is liberating. While people may feel embarrassed about what they did not know, they also feel empowered to be positioned for change. But we've witnessed a disturbing trend: Sometimes a newly empowered learner turns to judge and shame someone who has yet to begin a learning journey. If you had the privilege of learning, why would you punish someone for not having that privilege? How is it that a bud, who was graced with a teacher (e.g., guide, courses, books learning experiences) shows no grace toward a seed? This behavior is the antithesis of justice and belonging.

Shaming people for not knowing what you just learned feeds resistance. Furthermore, intentionally crafting learning experiences to be intense, painful, and shameful is an indication that you are attempting to perform a perverted version of antiracism and have not embodied justice and belonging. Compassion and grace are central to this work.

Finally, we've witnessed that cancel or call-out culture has caused our students to be stressed out about saying the wrong thing or asking the wrong questions in our classrooms. Cancel or call-out culture is the contemporary practice of exerting social pressure to boycott socially immoral views and actions. As parents and teachers, our children need to be able to be vulnerable with us. They need to be able to ask questions, be curious, and take risks. As we build racial competence, let's not become less humane.

Imbalanced Teaching

Recently, I (Tehia) was in a panel talk and a question was posed to us:

> I'm a seventh-grade Latina student in middle school, and I asked my teacher if we were learning about the Latinx Heritage this month 'cause it's Latinx Heritage Month. She said that it will cause problems between White and Latinx students, so we are sticking to the normal curriculum and not doing critical race theory. Is learning about my heritage in school critical race theory? And why is critical race theory a bad thing?

All of us on the panel were disappointed that this student's teacher did not take advantage of the opportunity to intentionally cultivate respect and value for cultural difference. It was a missed opportunity to cultivate respect and value not just for the Latinx student but also to strengthen the social relationships among the class. The student wanted historical validation. All students would have benefited from learning about Latinx people, contributions, and influences. The teacher did not see the value in building a shared racial, ethnic, and cultural understanding. Or perhaps the teacher felt unprepared to teach about the heritage, traditions, perspectives, histories, and lived experiences of Latinx groups.

When we don't feel equipped, we can admit that. We can affirm the student's request and then work with the student or student's parents to outline a plan of study. We can then set aside time to learn and create a plan to infuse lessons. All students will benefit from this expanded content.

In another instance, a few years ago, I had my most racially and culturally diverse undergraduate child development class. Typically, elementary education majors are predominantly White women who are monolinguistic and middle class. But this class included men and students of color who were also diverse in their experiences. Like every other semester, I spent time building community with them, and them with one another. We laughed, we learned, we raged at the racism in schools. One day, the students of color told my colleague, Dr. Miller, "Both you and Dr. Glass are teaching about race and racism and are trying to convince the White students that equity is important and valuable. But what are you teaching us [students of color] about ourselves?"

Dr. Miller and I agreed with the students. We were so focused on helping White students build their capacity to cultivate just and belonging classrooms that we had not dedicated time to affirming our students of color. Dr. Miller and I made a shift. We began to invest time and attention to affirming and validating by explicitly detailing the contributions, brilliance, and resilience of BIPOC. We also implicated systems even more. What I appreciate about this group of students is that they were comfortable "calling us in." We are in community with one another, so I need to do what is best for all of us.

Valuing Ideology over Empathy

We tell our children that it's easy to like someone who is like you. And for us adults, it's easy to hear someone whose ideology is like ours. But do we know how to hear someone with whom we do not agree? When we make space to listen, we can appreciate someone's biography over their ideology. We don't have to agree, but we can empathize.

During our foundation-building year, a teacher's religious perspective made it impossible for her to accept the science we were sharing. Although we did not agree with her perspective, we valued her and accepted that her perspective was valid and meaningful to her. Ultimately, we all shared in the desire and responsibility to participate in making our learning community better.

Ignoring How Children Experience Race/ism

Children's natural curiosity plus adult indifference and silence equals missed opportunities. Researchers and child developmentalists say that children are naturally curious. Asking questions is how they make sense of their world. In my (Tehia) TED Talk, *Conversations That Cultivate Seeds of Curiosity* (2022), I shared how adults ask, "How do we respond to our children when they ask about the injustices they experience, see on the news, or talk about in conversations with their friends?" We should not wait for kids to see something or experience something before we are forced to have a conversation about it, nor should we silence them with our silence. The evidence-based education about race that we offer children should cultivate seeds of curiosity in a way that encourages them to learn about self, history, systems, and actions. We have an opportunity to foster curiosity, inquiry, and critical thinking. As we work toward justice and belonging, let's equip our children to do the same.

Consider the conversations you are having with our children. Are you creating a space at home and in your classrooms where students see the value in one another—a space where the dignity of students is preserved and maintained. As we were writing this book, my first-grade son was told by a White classmate, "We don't want to play with you because your skin is brown." Three weeks prior, my son was told by another White schoolmate, "I don't like Black people. All of y'all are bad."

Fortunately, my partner and I have prepared our sons for this type of ignorance and harm. It's sad and infuriating that we have to do this. Because we already affirm him in the beauty and wonderful legacy of Blackness, we hope it did not impact him the way it could have.

Because White parents and teachers do not equip White children to be antiracist, we parents of color have to prepare our children to experience interpersonal racism. And when confronted about the racism their children exhibit, White parents respond with, "I don't know where they got that from!" One, this is not a helpful response. And two, the research on how children develop racial identity and racialized norms is clear about how children by the age of 7 can mirror social biases. We shared this research in Chapter 1. Phillip Goff and his research team in 2014 shared that children of color are racially dehumanized and traumatized inside and outside of school. This must end!

Bystander

Bystanding is when harm is being committed but no one steps in to stop the harm or help the victim. Bystanders assume that, at the moment, it is not their responsibility to step in and help. Some bystanders may approach the victim later and offer an apology for what happened to the victim or what was observed. However, an apology or a judgment about an incident or microaggression, for example, is not helpful. Instead such an act confirms that the bystander intentionally chose not to confront the offender.

"When no action is taken and people remain silent in the face of racism, it causes pain and suffering to the targets, it creates guilt in the mind of onlookers and it creates a false consensus that racism is OK," quoted by psychologist Dr. Derald Wing Sue in a 2020 *New York Times* interview by Ruth Terry. Our actions and specifically our inaction should never comply with racism or any type of social injustice. As you build racial competence, indignities and injustices that may have gone unnoticed before will become glaringly visible. When you see something, say (or do) something. Sometimes in the moment of harm, we don't know the best way to help. But you can at least discreetly do a small thing, like visible disapproval through body language.

You can plan and practice actions or words for when you observe disparaging behavior toward a group or person. Here are examples we've either used or seen others use:

- Stop, pause. This sets a boundary to define the harmful act or words.
- Show that you are confused by behavior—show that the behavior is not the accepted norm.
- Ask for clarity: What do you mean by that? Can you elaborate? Do you have facts to support your statement?
- Report the harm to the school, group or community leader, or classroom teacher.
- If a person is victimized, show them support and concern.

Not Noticing and Confronting White Supremacy Norms

Jones and Okun (2001) describe White supremacy norms as behaviors existing within an organization such as home or school, which acting as culture enforces adaptation or conformity. White supremacy norms are not solely perpetrated by White people. BIPOC can be informed by and exhibit White supremacy normative behavior as well. Here are some of the norms that Jones and Okun list:

- Perfectionism
- Sense of urgency
- Defensiveness
- Valuing quantity over quality
- Prioritizing the written word over oral and other forms of communication
- Denoting one right way
- Paternalism
- Either/or binary perspectives
- Power hoarding
- Fear of open conflict
- Individualism over collective identity
- Objectivity
- Possessing the right to comfort

Often these norms serve as primary assumptions, premises, and the standard by which other cultures and values are measured. Leaving White supremacy norms unchallenged and unchecked will make it almost impossible to cultivate justice and belonging. Jones and Okun offer ways to expand our perspectives and experiences beyond these norms to see the dignity and value of people and cultures that are not organized by White supremacy.

During a professional development (PD) break, a few teachers walked up to me (Tehia) and began talking negatively about the children in their classes—lack of parental support, the children's' neighborhoods, and lack of motivation. I responded by asking the teachers to elaborate on why they could not be culturally responsive. I asked them if the strategies were too complex or if there was something in particular that they didn't understand or know how to do. I was trying to get the teacher to see their own resistance to being culturally responsive. They were placing the blame on students who they believed did not deserve culturally responsive classrooms and teachers.

White Tears

On the podcast *We Can Do Hard Things with Glennon Doyle*, Dr. Yaba Blay (2022) shares a powerful perspective about how White women often weaponize their tears. Blay regards *White tears* as a performance to avoid accountability—especially when accountability is needed. Crying can be a quick way to stop the momentum of a learning experience—during a personal or professional development session or in a real-life moment. White tears are not authentic cleansing tears. Instead, they demand that everyone stop what they are doing and engage in comforting them. Furthermore, Blay adds that comfort often does not look the same way for the BIPOC during such learning experiences. For example, when we Black women cry, often we are not perceived as worthy of sympathy. We want you to honor your genuine emotions. But consider how White tears may impact others. If you need to cry, perhaps you can dismiss yourself from the space so that the learning can continue. If you choose to remain in the public space, be mindful to not take attention away from the instruction and learning and place it on yourself. Oh—and when BIPOC women cry, show us love.

Thinking We're Done

We can pause. We can rest. We can recover. But we cannot stop. Cultivating justice and belonging requires commitment and consistency. The antiracism journey is lifelong. Gardeners reap a harvest from all their care—tilling the soil, planting, rooting, and blooming. Then the cycle begins again. Likewise, you will experience a harvest. You will see growth and change. Remember to acknowledge and celebrate. Then reset for a new cycle. One way to do this is to continue to invest in personal and professional development opportunities.

For example, our organization Brownicity.com hosts a learning community membership where learning content is regularly created and added online. EmbraceRace.org hosts monthly workshops for parents. Organizations like Facing History & Ourselves, the Abolitionist Teaching Network, and Learning for Justice host webinars. You can also look for local, in-person organizations that support ongoing growth. In our area, the Racial Equity Institute helps people and organizations who want to understand and proactively address racism in their organizations and communities.

* * *

We listened to Susan's story (shared at the outset of the chapter) in disbelief. We clearly saw how within systemic and cultural norms, her brother was discredited and devalued. As a child, not only was Susan forced to navigate education spaces that did not see her family as worthwhile, but she also had to develop skills and savvy to place herself on the pathway to college. She learned to become an advocate for herself. Susan is now a brilliant teacher whose respect for students and their families is informed by her painful past. She sees and values everyone. She even sees students who don't want to be seen. Although Susan was able to become a gift to teaching despite her family being devalued, we can't help but wonder what might have been if there had not been so many obstacles. Perhaps her brother and cousins would have realized their aspirations as well.

Reflection and Practice

REFLECTION

1. Reflect on the story of Susan, the high school teacher. Think back to when you were in school. How were certain students centered? How were certain students marginalized? What could parents, teachers, and teacher leaders have done to advocate for Susan, her brother, and male cousins? What weeds are present in Susan's story?

2. Can you resonate with any of the weeds listed in the chapter?

3. What other weeds not listed have you experienced or observed?

4. Now that you are cultivating justice and belonging, what no longer holds value? What can potentially stall growth?

5. What language can you use to call someone in, instead of calling them out?

6. If you make a mistake, what is your emotional plan?
   a. Who will you go to for support?
   b. What are your coping strategies?
   c. What will you say to students, parents, and administrators?
   d. How will you bounce back?

PRACTICE

Create a plan to weed out things in your sphere of influence that work against cultivating justice and belonging. Include things like units, lessons, books, language, phrases, posters, practices, attitudes, approaches, old ways of thinking, rules, and policies.

CHAPTER 8
BLOOM: Mature into a New Normal

"A flower does not bloom for itself, but for the world; do likewise."
—Matshona Dhliwayo, Zimbabwean philosopher

When the bud reaches maturity, it slowly unfolds and opens up—it blooms. When the bud blooms, it is ready to produce a new generation. Likewise, we begin to reap what we have sown.

With a healthy, sustainable growth process, we yield fruit. With patience, consistency, and persistence, we begin to bloom and mature into the achievement of our potential. Over time, our buds unfold to reveal the beauty of our growth process. As you bloom, *now* is a great time to ask the question that people often ask first: *What do I do next?*

You have established a new normal. Now you can continue to build on what you have. You have settled into a practice that is sustainable and expandable. Remember that the growth process is cyclical, recursive, and seasonal. There will be seasons when evidence of growth is visible and seasons that seem fallow. During the fallow seasons, remember that rest is essential to the growth process. Farmers don't plant the same crop year after year. Some crops take more from the soil than others, so a different crop is planted the following year to allow soil to recover.

* * *

Tiffany, White Mom of Four

Dear former self,

I am so proud of you for taking the step to learn some hard truths about the realities of racism in America. I know it has been earth shattering. You feel anxious with the realities you see, the system in place that disadvantaged some that you didn't know you were a part of. You feel like you want to scream it out and fix it all at the same time. You are mad you didn't know this, that things were hidden from you. Good, all good emotions that come from this realization. Now you are fueled to want to make things better, but you don't know where to begin. It feels like you are playing catch up so you are frantic to do something important now. Should I march in the streets? Should I go around telling everyone how they are wrong? What do I do now?

This feeling is the first wave of change, but it is not the change you think. You want external change quickly but what really is happening is an internal shift. A shift in the way you see the world that also changes the way you interact with it. You smile at people you may not have even looked at before. You choose to be okay going to a store where more people don't look like you. You had always considered yourself a loving accepting person but you realized there had been some bias in your actions. Now you walk through the world differently, but it doesn't feel like enough, right?

To your amazement, you will start to experience another shift—a shift in attitude toward you. You will see family and friends start to feel uncomfortable with your choices, your stance, your voice. You will start to feel distanced and muted, and wonder what happened. You will learn that your shift can feel threatening to people around you and the way their world works. You want to pull back the curtain, but they prefer to not look. This part is painful because it is from people you care about. You valued their opinions in the past. This will be a fork in the road where you have to choose to either return to how things were or pursue this new path. But you know you can't go back, you can't unsee. So, you keep moving forward, wondering if you will be able to make a difference.

I have good news: You will! You need to see it for the long slow shift, like changing the course of a river. But changes will happen, and it starts in your home and in you. You are going to reexamine the school you chose for your kids and realize it is teaching a narrow viewpoint. You will remove them from the school you once thought so highly of and put them elsewhere. You are going to encounter many chances to face your own implicit bias with your children watching. You will have them at a play place where you see a large bus of Black children arrive and you are suddenly gripped with fear. Knowing what you know, you will pause, examine the root of that fear and see it comes from your childhood, when your mother ushered you off quickly from a playground when the "rough kids" arrived. You see how it all connects to become an implicit bias passed down probably for generations and you choose to not act on it. Instead, you sit there and look at each of the kids that just joined the fun and see them as you do your own.

"You probably like books" you think as you look at a young girl. "You might like basketball with my son" at another, "you might like science" to a third quietly in your head. And you make the fear dissolve with the truth that these are just kids, and your kids are fine. In fact, they are playing together oblivious to the burden you just released. It will be things like this that become the way you start living an antiracism life. And that is going to make ripples of change everywhere you touch.

So former me, don't get discouraged that you don't see change happening quickly. You are not in charge of the whole system changing overnight but you will be in charge of your whole world shifting to align with what you now believe. You will set your kids up to not have the same misinformation to continue the lies. You will break the cycle.

Love,

Your slightly wiser self

* * *

We have had the opportunity to spend years consulting, coaching, guiding, and supporting parents, teachers, teacher leaders, and children in homes, communities, classrooms, schools, and districts. Here we share about the fruit of our collective labor—what happens when you invest in and commit to a process of growing over an extended amount of time. In this chapter, we are sharing our recommendations based on our work, observations, challenges, and wins.

Tehia

I received funding through an institutional grant I applied for that allowed me to conduct research on how teachers integrate antiracism into their curricula. The project ran for 2 years and allowed me to build teacher efficacy around developing lessons through an antiracism lens. The grant allowed teachers to attend a 2-day racial equity workshop sponsored by a community organization. Following the workshop, we spent a year expanding content knowledge, pedagogical skills, and building lessons.

Within the 3–4-hour monthly meetings, my graduate assistant and I presented content, led discussions, and dedicated time for teachers to create. Time for creating was essential and protected. The teachers and I set goals and used the dedicated time to work toward accomplishing the goals. Throughout the month, the teacher cohort and I communicated back and forth about the content, pedagogical ideas, and assessments among other topics. Each month, teachers built lessons and units.

In 3–6 months, teachers experienced a complete learning cycle:

1. They developed their content knowledge on a topic that piqued their interest (e.g., the Reconstruction Era).
2. They designed a lesson or unit.
3. They located resources to use for their lesson or unit.
4. They had their lesson reviewed by a teacher in the cohort.
5. They had their lesson reviewed by me.

The teacher then taught their lesson to their students as I or the graduate assistant observed. Once we completed the cycle, we began all over again. That cycle occurred over the course of a school year. However, depending on the school or district, the cycle can take place in the summer. Teachers were compensated and supplied with the resources they needed. Teachers received classroom coverage so that this work could be done during the school day instead of after school.

As Teachers Bloom

As you create great lessons, use language that addresses and names race and antiracism. In a case during a professional development (PD) cohort, the teacher's lesson plan was thorough and included indicators of teaching historical accuracy. However, the conversation between student and teacher fell short. When learning about systemic injustice, the students asked a question, and the teacher's response did not provide clarity. For example, as she taught about the Civil Rights Movement, the teacher gave them the task of reading a children's book that represents that time period. Then they had to complete a sheet where students wrote facts about what they learned. At the end, there was a conversation between the class and the teacher in which the student asked why the White man was mean to Dr. King. The teacher framed the response around the idea that everyone should be kind to one another. By not explicitly naming how racism was a factor in how Black people were treated during the civil rights era, the teacher left space for the students to believe individual harm or bad behavior was the issue, instead of America's systemic and institutional oppression of its Black citizens. The teacher missed an opportunity. Though during the lesson plan design phase, we talked explicitly about how to name and talk about racism, this teacher reflected a low sense of efficacy.

Regarding teaching any topic, but especially antiracism, when a teacher's sense of efficacy or confidence is low, my data shows the following is present:

- ◆ Content delivery lives outside of the teacher. The lesson is delivered by a book, documentary, or website, for example, and becomes the driving source of information for the lesson.
- ◆ There is less teaching engagement and discussion about the content and more delivery of the instruction for a task to complete.

- Reflection or a synthesis of the lesson is missing, so students do not have an opportunity to share what they learned, and therefore the teacher does not have the opportunity to correct possible misinformation.
- A connection between historical and contemporary events is lacking, which prevents students from seeing relevance in what they are learning.

There is no book, documentary, or other video that can teach the full and complete lesson without you. Technology and activities cannot replace you as the teacher, for any content area—especially antiracism. You are there to facilitate learning and to fill in the gaps for your students. As the teacher, you must fully understand the content for yourself so you can scaffold your students. If you don't fully understand the topic or content, how will your students?

Even when you get content online, you should be prepared to fill in gaps for your students. There are not many commercial resources that address race, racism, and antiracism within the lessons. However, whatever you have or obtain, you will likely need to add the content that is missing from the prepackaged curriculum. You will also need to anticipate questions students may have, as well as be comfortable with explicitly answering them. If you are uncomfortable with the questions students are asking, here are a few responses you can use:

- I need to think about that more (then write the question down so you can respond later).
- Let's unpack that question, can you elaborate (if you don't understand what they're asking)?
- Let's write down all the questions we have so I can organize them, then talk about them tomorrow.

When you build your racial competence, your confidence for having conversations about race in your classrooms will increase. One high school teacher said, "The more I do it, the better I get!" In another example, a colleague who teaches math education wondered about how he could teach about justice and belonging as a White, cis male with young boys. He started small. One day in his primary mathematics class, instead of using generic data for the students to work on their math skills, he used data on race and policing. He wrote:

> I had what I think was the most authentic conversation about race and police and math yesterday in class that I've been able to have. I still have a LONG way to go in learning to build spaces for courageous conversations, but I got feedback especially from my Students of Color that it was appreciated. And I couldn't have gotten even this far without you.

This reiterates that creating space and time for teachers to learn, think, and act not only increases efficacy but also positively impacts students. Because he is a part of a learning crew that meets often to read and discuss articles, conduct a book study, or just be in conversation with one another, growth occurs individually and collectively.

Unlike this math teacher, many teachers end up avoiding a topic or content altogether, which contributes to the miseducation of young people. We have to move past the fear and equip children to critically think and disrupt injustice when they see it. In his 2018 book *Not Light, but Fire,* educator and author Matthew Kay points out that because of their identities, many children hear the conversations or are living in that "uncomfortable" realm. Therefore, they can handle uncomfortable topics and books. Although we may be afraid or underestimate our young people, we still need to teach an American history complete with Black history, Native American history, women's history, queer history, and disabled history.

One teacher taught a lesson on WWII but focused on the Black military members. In the lesson, the teacher showed how the Black military men were treated better in Europe than in their home country—the United States. When they returned home, the Black soldiers were treated terribly. A student said, "Why and how did this happen? Why haven't I learned about this sooner?" We need to be willing and prepared to teach about our country's massacres—both historical and contemporary. We need to teach about wars, government, and capitalism. We need to teach about organizing, activism, joy, and resilience. This is our reality, our lived experiences; therefore, we should help children to think critically about them as well.

You can begin with one book, one topic, one anchor concept or idea. Move from idea to lesson. You aren't going to be able to do it all right now or today. We recommend starting small, be okay with trial and error, and then see how the outcome feels. How did it feel to teach that content? How did your students respond? Build your personal confidence in taking risks with new content. Unpack where you will start. As an example, let's start with how we celebrate Dr. Martin Luther King, Jr. We often use a very sanitized version of Dr. King. Once we build our own knowledge base of who he was, we realize he was much more than his "I Have a Dream" speech. As you build your content knowledge about a more expansive understanding of Dr. King, use these questions to guide you:

- Whose voice is present? Whose voice is missing?
- What story is being told? Is it a complete story?
- What perspective is the content being told from?
- What questions have you prepared for your students?
- What questions can you anticipate from your students?

Read Dr. King's *Letters from a Birmingham Jail, Why We Can't Wait,* and *Where Do We Go from Here* as primary texts to understand how he felt. In most curricula available, we aren't taught about his brilliance, how he attended college at 16, and how he had a whole team who supported his work. One important part of his team was a gay man, Bayard Rustin. We aren't taught about how Dr. King had many Black celebrities who supported his work, or the close relationship he had with Malcolm X. We aren't taught about the intentional disruption of his movement by J. Edgar Hoover, the Federal Bureau of Investigation, and their COINTELPRO (Domestic Counterintelligence) program. Learn more about how to expand your MLK lessons by reading *As You Prepare to Celebrate Dr. King* (2022) on Brownicity's website.

We can expand our resources to ensure we provide students with a narrative that allows who we are learning about to be seen in their humanity. Gholdy Muhammad's (2020) book *Cultivating Genius* provides a great equity literacy framework and acknowledges the brilliance that already resides in teachers and students. The equity framework includes identity development, skill development, intellectual development, and criticality. Muhammad's framework provides a lens to explore all of Dr. King and other topics, not just the mainstream perspective that is often and easily shared.

During the first year of the grant-funded research project (2018–2019), one teacher shared that for her curriculum revision she wanted to expand her Greek civilization unit. We had lots of conversations about multiple perspectives and historical accuracy, which allowed her to see the narrow scope of her unit. She realized she needed to include African, Indigenous, Latinx, and other civilizations, which would be time intensive. Because that unit was upcoming and would take more time than she had, she decided to go in a different direction. She landed on a unit about activists. Her list of activists was diverse in its approach to race, geography, linguistics, age, gender, and interest.

The teacher had her students draw names of activists and then research them, create a poster, and present their findings to the class. After all the presentations were complete, the teacher displayed the posters outside the classroom. The next day, the poster of Claudette Colvin, a pioneer of the Civil Rights Movement, was vandalized. Someone drew and colored Colvin's lips as oversized and red, essentially making her look like a caricature from a 1920s Jim Crow minstrel shows. The teacher was furious and sprang into action. She threw out her plans for the day and taught a lesson on blackface and caricatures of Black people during Jim Crow. She helped her students understand why it was wrong to draw exaggerated features on the poster and shared the historical terror behind their actions. It took work for the teacher to pivot and use the unexpected incident as a reason to go deeper. She not only had to make the time to learn more about Jim Crow Minstrel shows but also had to prepare herself for the potentially awkward conversation about it. Did she have to do it? Absolutely! It is a disservice to stay silent when we see racism pop up in our classrooms. She was not a bystander that day. This is justice in action.

Efficacious educators:

- ◆ Take risks with the content and with their students. They are willing to discuss topics that are not status quo and allow their students to also be experts or designers of instruction.
- ◆ Facilitate lessons with content continuity. There is a more organized series of lessons around antiracism versus the additive "special lesson" that is taught once and is fragmented from the rest of the curriculum being taught.
- ◆ Challenge students with what they have learned and connect it directly to how they treat themselves and others.
- ◆ Make the content relevant, meaningful, and useful.

WHEN (NOT IF) YOU GET WEARY

Lessons are going well, you're learning so much new content, and you and your students are flourishing. Things can go well, *and* you can be tired. Looking historically at social movements across time, there are moments of ebb and flow. There are times when rest is needed. We want to normalize rest as a part of the process for doing justice work. Reflecting on opportunities for rest, restoration, and considering opportunities for mental health wellness while doing justice work is equally important. Social psychologist and professor Jennifer Eberhardt says in her 2019 book, "Change requires a kind of open-minded attention that is well within our reach." It is our hope that after reading this book your attention has become more open-minded and it leads to change, which is within your reach.

Working toward justice can be emotionally, cognitively, and psychologically exhausting. Unpacking your experiences, learning new information, then applying it is hard work. You will want to stop, but go back to your "why" that you reflected on in Chapter 1. You picked up this book and read it for a reason. Go back to that reason. Is your why for your children, your students, your colleagues, your community, the world? In those moments of weariness, remember what you are trying to improve.

You cannot do this work alone; you need your community to help you bloom. Even in a community, you may get lonely, but you aren't alone. Your crew will help you keep going. We are not the first to do this work of educational progress, and we won't be the last. But we are a part of the growth process of helping children to make the world better than we gave it to them. To see young people use their voice and be confident in their skin is one of the more rewarding experiences that we carry with us every day. We imagine every household, every classroom where young people are critical thinkers, and we see the value of their peers. We believe the return on that investment is infinite.

To acknowledge the weariness that may show up at some point, we want to check in to ensure you have some supports in place to help you thrive. Some of these recommendations we have already discussed but want to emphasize their importance.

Gather a crew. Who are your sounding boards? Who are the folks you can vent to without fear of judgment? Who will remind you of how awesome you are? Who will read the email response before you send it? Who are you planning with? Who are you dreaming with? When something goes wrong, who will be there to pick you up, dust you off, and remind you of your why? When you are tired, and someone in your crew is not, you rest and let them move the work forward. Once you are rejuvenated, you jump back in. You need these people in your life if you want to be able to sustain this work of dismantling the racism stronghold in homes and schools.

A therapist can be a great asset as a part of your crew. We discussed the importance of therapy in Chapter 4 with BIPOC, but it applies to White people as well. We've witnessed some of our White peers abandon their growth process, not because they did not want to cultivate justice and belonging, but simply because they were mentally and emotionally exhausted and did not access a therapist to process what they were going through. There will be times where you are triggered and you have no idea why. Something in your own life has bubbled up and has caused you to react in a way that may not support progress toward antiracism. Have a person who can guide and support you through this heart and emotional work. We spend lots of time learning our students' triggers, but do we know our own? Are there phrases or behaviors that cause us to disconnect from our students? Therapists can help you see patterns and be a neutral sounding board as you process your experiences.

In our experience, there is an ebb and flow to this work. There are times when the energy is high, and most are committed to revising the lessons or the curriculum. The money shows up, the resources are bountiful, and the kids are engaged in the content you're delivering. Then, there are times when the political landscape causes folks to be fearful about doing what's right. There is no money or time to revise the lesson or the curriculum, you spend more time online trying to curate your own resources, and your administrators feel the pressure of external stakeholders (school board members, parents, donors, and even the media) to not support you. We have seen this happen many times. And our advice is to keep going. Remember your why. Do what you know how to do in your classroom and be brave. Being brave is feeling scared but doing it anyway.

Given that we just told you to pause and rest, it may sound like we're contradicting ourselves when we tell you to keep going. When you need to pause and rest, *pause and rest*. You cannot pour from an empty cup. You have to be aware of your pause and rest point. When we are depleted, our patience is limited. We are less creative and innovative, and it is even more difficult to learn new information. Be aware of when you are at that point, and let your crew know. Then rest.

There was a day when I (Tehia) was working virtually with middle school and high school teachers over the summer, and I noticed early on their energy was low. I normally do a check-in with them—ask how they are doing and pose a warm-up question—and I could not get this normally chatty and close-knit group to talk. Even through the computer, I could see that they were tired. We were a year into the pandemic, and they were drained. I asked them a follow-up question, and they confirmed my hypothesis. At that moment, I threw away my plan to discuss language arts and racial literacy and instead focused on their well-being. I went through a couple of breathing exercises, we listened to some meditative music, and spent time journaling as a group for a few minutes to listen to their bodies and their brains, and their feelings. Once they were able to tap into their feelings and release some of that energy, we were able to work—on them. We began with naming what was going on at school and brainstorming some ways to take care of their students, themselves, and each other. We spent time discussing the ways that mental health and social emotional learning is relevant and aligns to justice, and how to incorporate more of it into our classrooms. We also spoke about how the district can do more mental health check-ins and support for teachers. Our conversations drifted into the racial reality for our students, dealing with the ongoing, state-sanctioned murder of Black people, the pandemic, ways to find joy, new restaurants, and everything in between. We breathed, we talked, we cried. By the time our 2 1/2 hours were done (I asked them to take the last 30 minutes to do something for themselves), we felt better, were less stressed, and were reminded that, just like our students need a break, so do teachers. And what they learned was sometimes you have to press pause on a lesson and attend to the needs of self and students. This may not have a standard connected to it, but it was equally important.

As Teacher Leaders Bloom

Recognize that educators need time to learn, think, and process rather than being catapulted into integrating new content and practices. Teachers need time to practice what they have taken time to learn in the PD or participate in one that includes time *within* the PD to learn, think, and work. The work of justice and belonging cannot be solely shouldered on educators. They are already tired and overworked with not enough time to accomplish everything. Committing to justice means that you must nurture your educators and create a space for them to bloom. When educators are provided time to do this work and have time to attend to what is important, they are able to accomplish great things. Educators are professionals and like any other profession should get what they need to be successful and carry out the mission of the school. As we maintained throughout the book, this work takes time—time to learn and process what was learned, reflect on how to integrate into the curriculum, pedagogically deliver, and design success.

Also, teacher leaders, do you have a plan and protocol for how you will respond to resistant educators, parents, or other constituents? How will you protect your educators who are aligning with the vision for justice and belonging? When the email or phone call comes from the disgruntled parent, what is the protocol for response? Consider educating the parent about the values and mission of the school, talk to both the teacher and student to get their sides of the story. By default, many of us do not want conflict and unintentionally throw our colleagues under the bus to appease someone who opposes antiracism in classrooms.

Shifting institutional and leadership responsibilities to individuals without vision, direction, or support is harmful and irresponsible. A culture shift requires feedback and commitment from parents, teachers, teacher leaders, and the community. Often, individuals—even children—are left to confront and dismantle institutionalized behaviors and practices. In this common scenario, individuals may have a lot of passion but very little knowledge or experience. In Chapter 4, we addressed how BIPOC may be expected to do all the heavy lifting and emotional labor for educating while White people settle for being sidekicks. Or White people with the best intentions may slide into the White savior trope. With one new charter school, the mostly White board designed the school from the ground up. There were lots of listening meetings, but the community was not really involved in the meetings. This was brought to their attention but was dismissed.

Wanting to ensure that the teachers were thinking about and acknowledging ways to disrupt racial harm that had been done to students of color in schools, a colleague reached out to this school to ask about teacher interview questions. Hours were spent curating questions that we thought would ensure they hired racially competent and exceptional teachers. Ultimately, our questions were disregarded, and deficit ideologies exist at that school. There was a prime opportunity for a culture shift, but leaders chose not to take advantage of it. Furthermore, they asked a BIPOC to spend time composing questions, then completely disregarded those questions. It was clear the mostly White board had preconceived notions about the populations of students, and the White savior mentality became part of the school culture.

Schools may have a statement of valuing diversity, or even a statement prioritizing antiracism, but those statements must show up in the school culture. We stated in earlier chapters that performative behaviors have no place in antiracism. You have to decide what your position will be before a situation arises. Educators are harmed when there is no prerequisite work done to prepare for protecting them, in which case teachers are left to defend themselves. That is a surefire way to reduce the morale in a school, and leave educators scared of what to teach. That is the antithesis of what should be happening in schools where antiracism is a priority or deemed valuable. If teachers are upholding the mission and values of the school, support them in doing so.

Educators must be compensated and supplied with the resources they need to be successful. Compensation may be:

- Class coverage (so this work can be done during the school day and not after school)
- Payment
- Content area books (to build your content knowledge)
- Web access to a resource
- Conference attendance
- Mentoring
- Other needs that can be negotiated between teacher and administrator

Resources for your instruction can include classroom books, teaching supplies, subscription services directly tied to instruction, or other needs decided by the teacher. There is a distinct difference in our opinion between compensation and resources. Compensation adds to teachers' skill sets and professionalism, and resources allow teachers to teach more effectively. Both are needed.

As Parents Bloom

Reading Tiffany's letter to her former self illuminates the hard work and time that has to occur at home. Reflect on what you've learned so far, and consider ways to share the content with your kids. Jennifer Harvey's 2018 book *Raising White Kids: Bringing Up Children in a Racially Unjust America* gives insight on how to have conversations with your children as well as the other adults in your life who may (or may not) be on this journey. What have you learned that you can share with your children? What books, shows, documentaries, or moments can you experience with them, then unpack what you all know to ensure you are opposing racism?

Additionally, parents, this is also a great time to discuss how you can support your teachers. They are in schools risking their own livelihood to embody what we have been talking about in this book. Let your child's teacher *know* you are there to support them as they build the capacity for all children to be in a space that is just, and where all children belong. Begin with one email, phone call, or visit at the beginning of the school year or even before it begins. Here is an example email you can craft to make your own:

> Dear [Insert teacher name],
>
> I am [your name here], the caregiver of [your child's name]. I want to take a moment to let you know that we uphold the ideals of [school name], school where diversity, equity, and inclusion are valued [or whatever statement may be in the mission statement or value system]. In our home, we are working to help my child/ren understand what justice means and how it looks in our everyday lives, which means we discuss race explicitly. I want you to know that my family and I are here to support your endeavors to teach the students in your class about the world they live in so they are prepared to function in it. Here are a couple of websites I follow that help adults support children in developing racial literacy: [Brownicity and EmbraceRace—are examples, insert your resources]. Please let me know how I can support you in your classroom. I am happy to volunteer when I can.
>
> In unity,
> Family [Family Name]

You can send the email at the beginning of the year, but your work as a parent does not end there. You may also need to send a similar email to administrators. They need to know what you are expecting to happen in their classrooms. The sole risk of discussing justice should fall not just on the teacher but on the administrator as well to support teachers. Other actions we can take to support your child's teacher throughout the year is to:

- Send in books they can use
- Send in gift cards so they can purchase the books they need
- Use your social networks to connect them to people who have expertise or experience that can be used in the classroom

Most teachers are not getting all of the materials they need to teach their students. Most schools are cash strapped and have limited resources so may not see the value in purchasing books that address race. Many teachers are purchasing these items out of their own pockets. We are sure that you know that teachers are *severely* underpaid and are doing a lot of the justice work on their own time, which they are *not* being compensated for. If financial support is not an option, send in websites, documentaries, podcasts, or other digital resources you may find. Consider creating an electronic list of all the resources you find with your teacher so you have a shared document you both can access.

When your child comes home and they are so excited about what they learned or how what they learned was just put into action, please share those moments with both the teacher, and the school administrator. *Teachers need to be affirmed, validated, and celebrated for teaching for justice and belonging!* Similar to parenting, teaching is delayed gratification. Teachers, like parents, need to know about those moments when students experience them. Those moments are confirmation that we are on the right track. We need to see those sprouts!

Other actions we can take to support our teachers and leaders include:

- Attending school board meetings so you can stay in the loop of what is going on
- Emailing the school board members when they are proposing oppressive actions
- Joining your PTA

Yes, these recommendations are time intensive, but you don't have to do them all. Do not forget your crew. One parent can attend school board meetings, one can be on the PTA, one can send emails, and another can curate the resources list. Gather this crew and talk about what each of you have learned, and how to support one another. The people who want to suppress learning about race/ism in the classroom brazenly take up political arms in order to do so. Those of us who know that teaching and learning about race/ism propels us toward cultivating justice and belonging need to proactively, strategically, and boldly show up in political spaces so that our position is known. Our motivation to act should not be in response to fear tactics, but a move inspired by our heart for humanity and supported by evidence-based research.

The New Normal

You've got this! Take this journey moment by moment, day by day, month by month, year by year.

Tehia

I have been working with a local school district for several years on their text equity within their elementary English language arts curriculum. We began with working with classroom and school libraries. I wanted to make sure the books on the shelves and in the students' hands offered the windows and mirrors we discussed in earlier chapters. Then we moved to classroom lessons. One teacher created an assignment where students had to find someone who made an impact on the United States that reflects their culture, race, or heritage. The teacher's rubric had the students' name contributions and also how they were oppressed by an -ism. The teacher intentionally did not want students just to celebrate but also to name the hardships and identify the systems that caused the hardships. Another elementary teacher said, "Each month I am more engaged with learning more ways to improve my lesson plans with a cultural responsive text equity approach." That excited me because I hear the increased sense of efficacy in their comments. After meeting with the group in January to prepare for Black History Month, I asked them in March how their Black History Month lessons went. One teacher said:

> They really enjoyed it. They had never heard of Marian Anderson, but knew the author of the book because it was the same as *Esperanza Rising,* which we had read earlier in the year. They knew Jackie Robinson, and baseball was high interest for some of them. They also got really excited to make connections to the picture books that we had read throughout the year and identify challenges that other people had overcome in their stories.

The teacher helped the students make connections to their schema via the author and a previous story they read and used their interest areas to make the learning relevant to them. I was excited for the students. A highlight of my career is watching these same elementary teachers who attended my PD cohort discuss on a local news segment (about children and race) how they are ensuring text equity is present in their classroom every day.

Now we have expanded to working with middle school and high school ELA (English and language arts) and English as a second language (ESL) teachers on curricular planning with text equity in mind. They are doing phenomenal work. They have vertically aligned instruction for Grades 6–12 so all ELA teachers can see what diverse anchor texts are being read, how it aligns to Learning for Justice's social justice standards, and what activities and assessments will occur. See Appendix E for the Content Analysis document. They are doing powerful things, and I'm so fortunate to be the facilitator of it. Our next step in the PD process is to observe one another teaching the lessons designed for text equity. They want opportunities to learn from each other because the teacher brilliance is in the classroom next to and across from them. There is nothing more rewarding than seeing the blooms.

Similar to this school district who prioritized justice and belonging, it is up to us to define and create just and belonging spaces. As designers of education, we consider the whole learning process—attention, memory, language, processing and organizing, writing, and higher-order thinking. These components interact not only with each other but also with emotions, classroom climate, behavior, social skills, teachers, and family. We then align strategies and tactics. Mismatching a strategy yields no gains, frustrates students and teachers alike, and fails to produce the desired result. For example, educators know that stress, shame, guilt, fear, and rage cannot teach, heal, or restore anything.

We don't have to cultivate and grow in silos. And we don't have to hide our growth. We can connect and join forces with like-hearted families, teachers, and schools. Families and communities riddled with apprehension and confusion about antiracism need to see your growth and hear your stories. Our fruit can help them understand that antiracism education is about liberation and transformation not just for some children, families, or schools but for *all* children, families, and schools.

We are saying it again for the people in the back: *Growth takes time*, so make time to grow into antiracism to cultivate justice and belonging. Aligning inner work and desire to see the fruit of our labor with the natural process for learning and growing will help stabilize us. We can be rooted in community with others, receive support, share best practices and avoidable missteps, and encourage one another. Recently, Brownicity was attacked on social media by a popular right-wing conservative group. A local noisemaker attempted to earn battle credit among her peers by making false claims about our intentions. Fortunately, we are seeded and rooted in a community—social and professional—where our work is notable and celebrated. The accusations hurt our feelings but did not pause our progress. As a matter of fact, people were concluding that Brownicity must be doing great work if this group has targeted us.

Reflection and Practice
REFLECTION
1. What in Tiffany's letter encouraged you? What made you nervous?
2. What is next for you as a parent, educator, or leader? How will you continue to use this book to support you in blooming—making your home, school, or classroom a more just and belonging space?

PRACTICE

1. Write a letter of commitment to cultivating justice and belonging for your home or classroom. Include a vision that centers antiracism. Include realistic goals for the next 5 years. List people and organizations with whom you will connect. Also, include encouraging words for yourself for those times you may get discouraged.

2. Craft a teaching statement that centers on justice and belonging for your children or students. Ask them what they need to feel like justice and belonging exists in their classroom and school or home.

Conclusion

*"They shall beat their swords into plowshares, and their spears into
pruning books"*
—Attributed to Isaiah, 8th-century BCE Israelite prophet

As parents, educators, scholars, creatives, and teacher leaders, we
are advantaged to strategically foster education that inspires a
culture of authentic liberation, justice, and belonging for all. But
because of the institutional inequality we've inherited, along with the
current resistance emboldened by White supremacy, actualizing such
a culture shift may seem impossible. So we have a choice: we can
either suppress growth to remain committed to disregarding race/
ism, or we can convert that energy into creating opportunities and
spaces where every child can be seen, safe, valued, and inspired.

We can choose to reconstruct resources once weaponized
exclusively to maintain White dominance (schools, curricula,
neighborhoods, churches, policy-making) into gardening tools to
uproot systemic inequality and cultivate transformation. We can
rebuild what racism has ruined. We can become known as repairers
of broken thinking and spaces, where no one is denied dignity and
where everyone can exhale and feel at home.

We don't have to pretend that growth occurs only during sunny
days, either. Rainy days, though less favorable, are necessary for the
seed's potential to be realized. As we've tilled and planted, we've
experienced many rainy days that feel like setbacks. Remember, a
setback can be a setup to come back and overcome. Did you know
that grass is greener after a thunderstorm? Grass needs nitrogen but
is unable to absorb it from the air. Rain forces nitrogen to the ground
where microorganisms convert it in the soil. During a thunderstorm,
lightning instantly creates nitrogen oxide, which grass absorbs
immediately without the help of microorganisms. Oftentimes,

overcoming obstacles requires us to invoke creativity, to change our thinking, and to shift our practices. You need both the sun and thunderstorms.

So that we don't quit, we can liken our growth to that of the Chinese bamboo tree. In its first year, the Chinese bamboo tree shows no visible signs of active growth. In the second year, there are no visible signs of growth above the soil. In year three, we see nothing. And in the fourth year, still nothing. At this point, we may wonder if the seed was rotten or perhaps the soil was rocky. We may begin to wonder if we have wasted our time and effort. Finally, in the fifth year, we begin to see the Chinese bamboo tree peeking through the soil. Then, the seed that we had almost given up on grows 80 feet in just 6 weeks (Morris, *How Success Is Like A Chinese Bamboo Tree*). During the 4 years it seemed to be dormant, the tree was actually developing a root system strong enough to support its potential for outward growth in the fifth year and beyond. Had the seed, soil, and root not developed a strong underground foundation, the Chinese bamboo tree could not have sustained its life as it grew.

The same is true of our growth. We must value and appreciate the early stages—understanding our environment, ourselves, our histories, and our potential. Skipping the groundwork forfeits and forsakes the bloom. Each stage of growth has something significant to offer.

Understandably, we are eager to shift our practices. Collectively, we want to be further along than we are. But we must consider where we are planted. It is unhealthy for someone who has embodied antiracism for decades to be compared with someone who is at the beginning of the lifelong learning journey. For example, as noted in Chapter 8, in the year following the groundwork year, some teachers chose to participate in the grant-funded professional development project. Though it included a 2-day intensive racial equity workshop and monthly support meetings, participating teachers still needed more time for what they learned to become a part of them. Because of how we learn, we need to intake, process, reflect, adjust, practice, and repeat over an extended period of time. We require time to settle into our new antiracist selves. Over time, as competence grows, confidence multiplies.

Because you are tilling soil, planting seed, and nurturing children, communities, and classrooms in ways that seem new, the unfamiliarity may feel overwhelming. Remember that you have committed to a growth *journey*, not a five-step production program. In order to embrace the journey,

1. Understand that you are endowed with growth potential.
2. Establish a long-term vision.
3. Set goals based on the growth stages that we have shared in this book.
4. Prioritize the vision and goals.
5. Trust your innate growth process. Though you may need to press *pause*, don't press *stop*. Don't press *fast-forward*.
6. Make time to become rooted or anchored.
7. Respect and commit to each growth stage.
8. See challenges as growth opportunities.
9. Express gratitude for growth.

We reap what we sow. Several generations passed between when Thomas Jefferson first *suggested* a theory of race in the United States (the seed) and when race became fixed and normalized within our national conscience (the harvest). We are now within the generation that is moving to understand how race/ism have worked against all of us. We are in a prime time for cultivating the just society we long for. If we are strategic, intentional, and committed, we will experience the bud bloom.

Social entrepreneur Trabian Shorters (2022) ended his *On Being with Krista Tippett* interview (February 3, Episode 1030) with this contextualized encouragement.

Tippett: . . .I've heard you say it, that we can flip the script in a short period of time and that new generations actually do have the capacity right now to change this narrative at scale.

Shorters: Well, let me maybe contextualize that a little bit. The baby boom generation, the civil rights generation, those folks have been adults for 50 years. Everything about our sense of policy and priorities, everything about our culture, has flowed through one generation for half a century. And they're aging out of institutional power. So as we experience that instability, the other thing that's going on simultaneously is the most diverse generation that we've ever had is becoming the mainstream. And that is why they're going to fundamentally challenge whatever existing narratives around what a gender is, what women's roles are, who is Black or White or whatever—even the way we think about race—how fluid those definitions—they're going to challenge all that, because it doesn't fit their experience.

So this is it. [laughs] This is the last time that one racial group can carry the majority of this democracy. And in that type of democracy—when you have racial pluralism, where there is no majority—then the skills to be able to see each other's value becomes a functional skill. It's not a nice one to have; it's the only way to govern.

Our children need us to equip them with such functional skills. They need us to plant seeds of justice and belonging. So, join us in the garden. And don't be afraid to get your hands dirty or be skeptical about wading in mud. Remember, the most beautiful flower, the lotus, roots itself and grows in the mud.

Appendix A: KWLH Chart to Explore Your Knowledge Base

Content Area/Topic

What do you KNOW?	WHAT do you want to know?	What did you LEARN?	HOW will you integrate it into your lesson?

Appendix B: Self-Care Plan

Detail what you can do to decompress/reflect in the allotted time.

Time Available	Activity	Resource Needed	Cost
5 minutes			
30 minutes			
1 hour			
3 hours			
6 hours			
24 hours			

Appendix C: Not Judging a Book by Its Cover: Social Justice Book Rubric

The purpose of this rubric is to assist you in selecting appropriate books that are social justice–oriented for your classroom. Examine the illustrations, peruse the text, and answer the questions.

Title _____

Author & Illustrator _____

Expertise: Describes the experience and knowledge the author and illustrator have so that they can create accurate portrayals of the people depicted.

---

1. According to the author/illustrator notes, is the author/illustrator qualified to write or illustrate material related to the book's theme? (*ex: they have experienced the subject of the book or conducted extensive research*)   Yes No

2. Has the book been recognized by an organization that highlights the work of multicultural literature? (*ex: The Coretta Scott King Award, New Voices Award*)   Yes No

3. Is the author representative of the racial group that is written about in the book? If not, do they have expertise on that racial group from an affirming perspective?   Yes No

Briefly explain your rationale:

Accuracy: A critical aspect of high-quality multicultural literature, it ensures that stereotypes are not perpetuated and that characters are portrayed realistically.

1. Does diversity exist among the members of each cultural group portrayed? *(ex: variety of careers held, variety of physical attributes, different social class)*   Yes No

2. Representation of people, events, places, and cultural artifacts is accurate and not distorted. *(ex: teepees are not houses for all Native Americans regardless of tribe)*   Yes No

3. Book includes significant specific cultural information, not just stereotypes. *(ex: Latinos are not categorized as the same; Mexican, Puerto Rican, Cuban, etc.)*   Yes No

4. Historical Information is correct.   Yes No

5. Are there multiple abilities represented? (Wheelchair, hearing impaired, neurodivergent, etc.)   Yes No

Briefly explain your rationale:

Respect: Author and illustrator show respect for the characters portrayed. They avoid the use of derogatory language and illustrations.

1. Do the author/illustrator avoid using condescending language and illustrations? Yes No *(ex: no words like savage, lazy, primitive, third world)*

2. Representation of characters is realistic. *(ex: there are no stereotypes in the characters' speech, appearance, and behaviors. No overemphasized facial features or characters look like caricatures)*   Yes No

3. Characters demonstrate awareness of identity, conflict, and/or pride associated with themselves and others.   Yes No

4. Words in foreign language are used and correctly spelled.   Yes No

5. Style of artwork/illustrations represented in books (graffiti, abstract, repurposed items in pictures, etc.).   Yes No

Briefly explain your rationale:

Message: The book shows acceptance of diversity, supports democratic values of equity, and addresses social and political issues responsibly.

1. Characters are portrayed as equal to mainstream groups. *(ex: characters of color are not portrayed as subservient or supporting characters)*   Yes   No

2. Wisdom is also held by characters of color. *(ex: characters solve their own problems versus relying on white characters to solve their problems)*   Yes   No

3. Social justice is addressed directly.   Yes   No

4. Languages used that are not standard American English. (prose, rap, poetry, metaphors, African American Vernacular English, spoken langugage talk)   Yes   No

5. Book positively impacts the reader (emotionally, cognitively, physically, etc.).

Briefly explain your rationale:

Quality: The book meets general quality standards applied to other books.

1. The story has a well-developed plot, is interesting, and engaging.   Yes   No

2. Illustrations have pleasing use of color, composition, and/or perspective.   Yes   No

3. Grammar and word choice are easily understood and age appropriate.   Yes   No

4. Informational texts are historically accurate and include multiple perspectives.   Yes   No

Briefly explain your rationale:

A book with mostly *yes's* can be considered appropriate; a book with several *no's* may not be appropriate. However, a book with one or two *no's* could still be used in your classroom as long as you discuss the problematic features with your students.

Total:

Overall Recommendation:

I would recommend this book.	Yes No
I would use this book.	Yes No
I have resources to support the gaps that may exist in this book.	Yes No

Resources to consider as a supplement to the book:

Questions to consider to support the book:

Comments:

Appendix D: Tatum Book Small Group Study Guide

Reading/Meeting Schedule
1. **Date and Time.** We will discuss parts 1–2 (pp. 1–90).
2. **Date and Time**. We will discuss parts 3–5 (pp. 93–219).

Before You Start Reading:
♦ Write your definition of racism. Then notice the differences/ similarities between how you define this word and the definition we are given in the first chapter of the book.

♦ What is a healthy racial identity? Who helped to form your sense of racial identity?

♦ Consider the people who have influenced you (parents, teachers, community) as well as society, strangers, media.

♦ How has stereotyping affected the way you see people, especially those who you classify as different from yourself?

After reading and before our meetings, reflect on the following questions in the book's ***Reader Discussion Guide*** (pp. 235–242): Numbers 1, 5, 9, 12, 15–19, 21–25.

Meeting 1 Agenda and Discussion Prompts
INTRO
♦ Damage of the legacy of silence (p. 36) – Comfort/Discomfort – Brave space

♦ Rhetorical Parachutes – (from *Racism without Racists,* Eduardo Bonilla-Silva)

PARTS 1–2

♦ Share your reaction to Tatum's definition of racism. How did it compare with yours? (p. 7)

♦ How does racism hurt White people? (p. 14)

♦ How am I participating in institutional racism without knowing it? (p. 43 – *Do I have to be Black?*) How did academic achievement become defined as exclusively White behavior? What is it about the curriculum and the wider culture that reinforces the notion that academic excellence is an exclusively White domain? (p. 64 and p. 18)

♦ Action: Develop a list of practical instructional strategies. As our awareness grows, what can we implement in our classrooms?
  • 3–5 min – quick write on this topic
  • Share ideas with your partner
  • Group share

♦ From the discussion guide in the back, Tatum writes, "We need to understand that in racially mixed settings, racial grouping is a developmental process in response to an environmental stressor."
  • Why is connecting with one's ethnic or racial peers important in the process of identity development, and why should it be encouraged? What are the primary advantages and disadvantages of such peer groups?

Meeting 2 Agenda and Discussion Prompts

Whole group – Identify where you are now in your thinking. What do you notice?

What continued thoughts have you had about racism? Prejudice? Racial identity development?

What do you notice now that you didn't before studying this book?

What conversations have you had that have stuck with you?

What new questions do you have?

Where are we individually?

     Turn and Talk

     White Identity Development:

1. Abandoning racism and recognition of and opposition to institutional and cultural racism
   a. Contact stage – little attention to racial identity (I'm just normal)
   b. Disintegration – growing awareness of racism and White privilege; often accompanied with shame, guilt, anger, growing contradiction of the idea of American meritocracy
   c. Reintegration – fear and anger at people of color b/c they must have caused the problem; seen as group member rather than individual; requires someone to point the way toward constructive action
   d. Pseudo-independent stage - intellectual understanding of racism as a system of advantage but doesn't know what to do about it; wanting to escape whiteness to embrace people of color
   e. Immersion/emersion – a need for other White people who are further along in the process to show the way; see Whiteness in a positive light; need for White allies
   f. Autonomy – positive feelings of Whiteness

2. Disintegration Stage
   • What elements and representation of institutional and cultural racism are observable today in the entertainment and news media and in our schools, corporations, government, and other institutions?
   • How might both people of color and White people call attention to these instances, work for their elimination, and establish non-racist and anti-racist representations and behavior?
     "How We Are Ruining America" NYTimes Opinion Article - David Brooks
   • Advantage given to upper-middle class students because families have the means and money to focus on the education and cultural, travel opportunities of that child – cultural experiences like unpaid internships, etc.

3. Immersion/Emersion stage
   • Tatum draws attention to the "history of White protests against racism, a history of Whites who have resisted

the role of oppressor and who have been allies to people of color" (p. 108).

- What parts of this history are you familiar with?
- What might be the benefits of learning more about that history?
- In what ways has that history provided, and might it now provide, models of thought, action, and cooperation for everyone? (list of historic allies p. 112)
- How do we take what we have learned about stages of racial development (Black and White) and use it to better understand/lead students to the next appropriate stage(s)?

4. **Next Steps**

What else can we do as a faculty to face and interrupt systemic/cultural racism?

Other Resources

Leading On Opportunity (https://leadingonopportunity.org/about/)

This is the Charlotte-Mecklenburg Opportunity Task Force that grew out of the report about upward mobility. A Harvard/UC Berkeley Study examined 50 cities' ability for people to move out of poverty and Charlotte landed number 50 out of 50 cities that were studied. This website houses the report they have issued which includes findings on impact of segregation, early childhood education, child and family stability, social capital, and next steps. The website also hosts a blog with some interesting articles, a list of upcoming events, and next steps as they see it.

Share Charlotte (https://sharecharlotte.org/) – This is a curated list of non-profit and volunteer organizations so that you can find the organizations that address what matters most to you. They help you connect to organizations through events, how to volunteer, donate, etc.

On the Table CLT (http://onthetableclt.org/) — On the Table CLT is an event sponsored by Foundation of the Carolinas. In an effort to help people within the Charlotte-Mecklenburg area connect around issues and needs in our area, small groups of people gather to share perspectives on issues around race, poverty, upward mobility, etc. There is a place to "join" the group to be kept up-to-date on plans. They are looking for hosts as well as members who want to join a discussion group for that day.

5. **Personal Exit Slip**
   - How will I continue my **professional** journey to explore my own racial identity and use what I know to interrupt systemic racism?
     - How will I continue my **personal** journey to explore my own racial identity and use what I know to interrupt systemic racism?

Appendix E: Content Analysis Chart

WEEK	Big Idea/ Theme/Topic/ Concept	Social Justice Standard (Learning for Justice)	ELA Instructional Practices (Disrupt Texts)	Essential Question	Diverse Anchor Text	Student Objective	Instructional Moves	Resources	Anticipated Student Questions	Assessment (What does success look like?)
1 Unit Zero										
2 Unit Zero										
3 Unit One										
4 Unit Two										

References

Chapter 1

Bigler, Rebecca S., Averhart, Cara J., and Liben, Lynn S. (2003). "Race and the Workforce: Occupational Status, Aspirations, and Stereotyping Among African American Children." *Developmental Psychology* 39, no. 3: 572.

Briscoe-Smith, Allison. (2008). "Rubbing Off." June 1. https://greatergood.berkeley .edu/article/item/rubbing_off

Dore, Rebecca A., Hoffman, Kelly M., Lillard, Angeline S., and Trawalter, Sophie. (2014). "Children's Racial Bias in Perceptions of Others' Pain." *British Journal of Developmental Psychology* 32, no. 2: 218–231.

Sealey-Ruiz, Yolanda, and National Council of Teachers of English. (2021). "Racial Literacy. A Policy Research Brief Produced by the James R. Squire Office of the National Council of Teachers of English." https://ncte.org/wp-content/ uploads/2021/04/SquireOfficePolicyBrief_RacialLiteracy_April2021.pdf

We Stories. *What We Know*. http://www.westories.org › what-we-know

Chapter 2

Agrawal, Radha. (2018). *Belong: Find Your People, Create Community, and Live a More Connected Life*. Workman Publishing.

Boyer, Ernest L. (1990). *In Search of Community*. ERIC Clearinghouse.

Cooper, Jewell. (2014) Incorporating Diversity into the Program [PowerPoint slides]. UNC Charlotte. Department Lecture.

Davis, Fania E. (2019). *The Little Book of Race and Restorative Justice: Black Lives, Healing, and U.S. Social Transformation*. Simon and Schuster.

Gooden, Mark Anthony. (2021). "Why Every Principal Should Write a Racial Autobiography." *Educational Leadership* 78, no. 7: 32–37. https://www.ascd .org/el/articles/why-every-principal-should-write-a-racial-autobiography

Jones, Camara Phyllis. (2000). "Levels of Racism: A Theoretic Framework and a Gardener's Tale." *American Journal of Public Health* 90, no. 8: 1212.

The Bible Project. (Oct 27, 2017). Justice [Video]. Youtube. https://youtu.be/ A14THPoc4-4

Zamalin, Alex. (2019). *Antiracism*. New York University Press.

Chapter 3

Eberhardt, Jennifer L. (2019/2020). *Biased: Uncovering the Hidden Prejudice That Shapes What We See, Think, and Do.* Penguin Books.

Glass, Tehia Starker. (2022). "Conversations That Cultivate Seeds of Curiosity." TED Talk. https://www.youtube.com/watch?v=BUfuqp1PnIQ

Hammond, Zaretta. (2015). *Culturally Responsive Teaching and the Brain: Promoting Authentic Engagement and Rigor Among Culturally and Linguistically Diverse Students.* Corwin Press.

Henriques, Gregg. (2014). "Cultural Bubbles in the Era of Globalization." https://www.psychologytoday.com/us/blog/theory-knowledge/201406/cultural-bubbles-in-the-era-globalization

Mayer, Richard E., and Moreno, Roxana. (1998). "A Cognitive Theory of Multimedia Learning: Implications for Design Principles." *Journal of Educational Psychology* 91, no. 2: 358–368.

Ormrod, Jeanne Ellis. (2013). *Educational Psychology: Pearson New International Edition: Developing Learners.* Pearson Higher Ed. https://www.cnn.com/2020/01/23/us/barbers-hill-isd-dreadlocks-deandre-arnold-trnd/index.html

Chapter 4

Anderson, Carol. (2016). *White Rage: The Unspoken Truth of Our Racial Divide.* Bloomsbury Publishing.

Anderson, Carol. (2021). https://www.vox.com/22243875/white-rage-white-nationalism

Baldwin, James. (1961). *Nobody Knows My Name: More Notes of a Native Son.* Dial Press.

Berry, Lucretia. (2016). *What LIES Between Us—Fostering First Steps Toward Racial Healing Journal and Guide.* CreateSpace Independent Publishing.

Brown, Brené. (2019). *The Call to Courage.* Documentary (Sandra Restrepo, director). Netflix.

Crenshaw, Kimberlé W. (2017). *On Intersectionality: Essential Writings.* New Press.

Dunbar-Ortiz, Roxanne. (2014). *An Indigenous Peoples' History of the United States.* Vol. 3. Beacon Press.

Fasching-Varner, Kenneth J. Albert, Katrice A., Mitchell, Roland W., and Allen, Chaunda. (2015). *Racial Battle Fatigue in Higher Education: Exposing the Myth of Post-Racial America.* Rowman & Littlefield.

Goff, Phillip Atiba, Jackson, Matthew Christian, Di Leone, Brooke Allison Lewis, Culotta, Carmen Marie, and DiTomasso, Natalie Ann. (2014). "The Essence of Innocence: Consequences of Dehumanizing Black Children." *Journal of Personality and Social Psychology* 106, no. 4: 526.

Hunt, Brittany D. (2020). "My Grandmother's Granddaughter: Indigenous Resilience." TED Talk. https://www.youtube.com/watch?v=h5TQSdgTgfQ

Loewen, James W. (1995/2008/2018). *Lies My Teacher Told Me: Everything Your American History Textbook Got Wrong*. New Press.

Love, Bettina L. (2019). *We Want to Do More Than Survive: Abolitionist Teaching and the Pursuit of Educational Freedom*. Beacon Press.

Michael, Ali. (2016). *Raising Race Questions: Whiteness and Inquiry in Education*. Teachers College Press.

Okun, Tema. (2000). "White Supremacy Culture." *Dismantling Racism: A Workbook for Social Change Groups, Durham, NC: Change Work*. http://www. dismantlingracism. org/Dismantling_Racism/liNKs_files/whitesupcul09. pdf

Powell, John Anthony. (2012). *Racing to Justice: Transforming Our Conceptions of Self and Other to Build an Inclusive Society*. Indiana University Press.

Singh, Anneliese A. (2019). *The Racial Healing Handbook: Practical Activities to Help You Challenge Privilege, Confront Systemic Racism, and Engage in Collective Healing*. New Harbinger Publications.

Chapter 5

Adichie, Chimamanda Ngozi. (2009). "The Danger of a Single Story." TED Talk. https://www.ted.com/talks/chimamanda_ngozi_adichie_the_danger_of_a_ single_story?language=en

Bishop, Rudine Sims. (1990). "Windows and Mirrors: Children's Books and Parallel Cultures." In *California State University Reading Conference: 14th Annual Conference Proceedings*, pp. 3–12. https://files.eric.ed.gov/fulltext/ ED337744.pdf

Tatum, Beverly Daniel. (1997/2017). *Why Are All the Black Kids Sitting Together in the Cafeteria?: And Other Conversations About Race*. Hachette.

Chapter 6

Berry, Lucretia. (2022). *Hues of You—An Activity Book for Learning About the Skin You Are In*. Waterbrook.

Katz, Karen. (1999). *The Colors of Us*. Macmillan.

King Jr., Martin Luther. (2010). *Where Do We Go from Here: Chaos or Community?* Vol. 2. Beacon Press.

Kissinger, K., Bohnhoff, C., Kissinger, K., and Kissinger, K. (2014). "All the Colors We Are: The Story of How We Get Our Skin Color= Todos los colores de nuestra piel: la historia de por qué tenemos diferentes colores de piel."

Tatum, Beverly Daniel. (1997/2017). *Why Are All the Black Kids Sitting Together in the Cafeteria?: And Other Conversations About Race*. Hachette.

Tillman, G., Jr. (2018). *The Hate U Give*. Twentieth Century Fox.

Chapter 7

Berry, Lucretia. (2022). *Hues of You—An Activity Book for Learning About the Skin You Are In*. Waterbrook.

Doyle, G. (Host). (2022, March 17). *The Power of Rethinking Everything with Dr. Yaba Blay: We Can Do Hard Things with Glennon Doyle* [Audio podcast]. Apple Podcasts. https://podcasts.apple.com/us/podcast/the-power-of-rethinking-everything-with-dr-yaba-blay

Glass, Tehia Starker. (2022). "Conversations That Cultivate Seeds of Curiosity." TED Talk. https://www.youtube.com/watch?v=BUfuqp1PnIQ

Goff, Phillip Atiba, Jackson, Matthew Christian, Di Leone, Brooke Allison Lewis, Culotta, Carmen Marie, and DiTomasso, Natalie Ann. (2014). "The Essence of Innocence: Consequences of Dehumanizing Black Children." *Journal of Personality and Social Psychology* 106, no. 4: 526.

Goodman, Alan H., Moses, Yolanda T., and Jones, Joseph L. (2019). *Race: Are We So Different?* John Wiley & Sons.

Hammond, Zaretta. (2015). *Culturally Responsive Teaching and the Brain: Promoting Authentic Engagement and Rigor Among Culturally and Linguistically Diverse Students*. Corwin Press.

Jones, Kenneth, and Tema Okun. (2001)."White supremacy culture." *Dismantling racism: A workbook for social change* https://www.whitesupremacyculture.info/

Ross, Loretta J. (2020). "What If Instead of Calling People Out, We Called Them In?" *New York Times*. https://www.nytimes.com/2020/11/19/style/loretta-ross-smith-college-cancel-culture.html

Terry, Ruth. (2020). "How to Be An Active Bystander When You See Casual Racism". *New York Times*. https://www.nytimes.com/2020/10/29/smarter-living/how-to-be-an-active-bystander-when-you-see-casual-racism.html

Chapter 8

Eberhardt, Jennifer L. (2019/2020). *Biased: Uncovering the Hidden Prejudice That Shapes What We See, Think, and Do*. Penguin Books.

Glass, Tehia Starker. (2022). "As You Prepare to Celebrate Dr. King." *Brownicity*. January 4.https://brownicity.com/blog/as-you-prepare-to-celebrate-dr-king/

Harvey, Jennifer. (2018). *Raising White Kids: Bringing Up Children in a Racially Unjust America*. Abingdon Press.

Kay, Matthew R. (2018). *Not Light, but Fire: How to Lead Meaningful Race Conversations in the Classroom*. Stenhouse Publishers.

King Jr, Martin Luther. (1992) "Letter from Birmingham jail." *UC Davis L. Rev.* 26: 835.

King, Martin Luther. *Why We Can't Wait*. (1963/1964/2000). Penguin,

King Jr, Martin Luther. *Where Do We Go from Here: Chaos or Community?* (1968/1986/2010). Vol. 2. Beacon Press,

Muhammad, Gholdy. (2020). *Cultivating Genius: An Equity Framework for Culturally and Historically Responsive Literacy.* Scholastic Incorporated.

Shorters, Trabian. (2022). "A Cognitive Skill to Magnify Humanity." Podcast (Chris Heagle, Producer). *On Being with Krista Tippett,* February 3. 50:44. https://onbeing.org/programs/trabian-shorters-a-cognitive-skill-to-magnify-humanity/

Conclusion

Morris. How Success Is Like A Chinese Bamboo Tree. Matt Morris. https://www.mattmorris.com/how-success-is-like-a-chinese-bamboo-tree/

Tippett, K. (Host). (February 3, 2022). A Cognitive Skill to Magnify Humanity. Episode 1030. [Audio podcast episode]. *On Being with Krista Tippett.* KTPP. https://onbeing.org/programs/trabian-shorters-a-cognitive-skill-to-magnify-humanity/

Resources

Chapter 1
BOOKS
Racing to Justice: Transforming Our Conceptions of Self and Other to Build an Inclusive Society by John A. Powell

ARTICLES
"5 Ways to Ground Your Teaching in Equity and Justice," https://facingtoday.facinghistory.org/5-ways-to-ground-your-teaching-in-equity-and-justice

"Does 'Belonging' Mean Economic Inclusion or New Economic Structures?" by Eli Moore https://belonging.berkeley.edu/blog-does-belonging-mean-economic-inclusion-or-new-economic-structures

"Children Are Not Colorblind: How Young Children Learn" by Erin Winkler https://www.academia.edu/3094721/Children_Are_Not_Colorblind_How_Young_Children_Learn_Race

TED TALKS BY PARENTS AND EDUCATORS
Children Will Light Up the World If We Don't Keep Them in the Dark by Lucretia Berry https://www.ted.com/talks/lucretia_berry_children_will_light_up_the_world_if_we_don_t_keep_them_in_the_dark

Cultivating Seeds of Curiosity by Tehia Starker Glass https://www.youtube.com/watch?v=BUfuqp1PnIQ

Chapter 2
ONLINE
"Foundations" (an online on-demand, self-paced introduction to antiracism course) by Brownicity.com, https://join.brownicity.com/courses/foundations

"White Supremacy Culture" by Kenneth Jones and Tema Okun, https://www.thc.texas.gov/public/upload/preserve/museums/files/White_Supremacy_Culture.pdf

"ABC's of Social Justice: A Glossary of Working Language for Socially Conscious Conversation by Department of Inclusion & Multicultural Engagement," Lewis & Clark College, https://college.lclark.edu/live/files/18474-abcs-of-social-justice

BOOKS

Why Are All the Black Kids Sitting Together in the Cafeteria by Beverly Tatum

So You Want to Talk About Race by Ijeoma Oluo

Me and White Supremacy – Combat Racism, Change the World, and Become a Good Ancestor by Layla Saad

I'm Still Here by Austin Channing Brown

Chapter 3

BOOKS

The Inner Work of Racial Justice – Healing Ourselves and Transforming Our Communities Through Mindfulness by Rhonda V. Magee

Culturally Responsive Teaching and the Brain by Zaretta Hammond

Biased by Jennifer Eberhardt

Culturally Responsive Teaching by Geneva Gay

The Racial Identity Handbook by Annelise Singh

White Rage by Carol Anderson

CHILDREN'S BOOKS

Hues of You – An Activity Book for Learning About the Skin You Are In by Lucretia Berry

Race Cars by Jenny Devenny and Charnaie Gordon

The Skin You Live In by Michael Tyler

M is for Melanin by Tiffany Rose

The Colors of Us by Karen Katz

Your Fantastic Elastic Brain by Joann Deak

Chapter 4
TED Talk
The Danger of a Single Story by Chimamanda Ngozi Adichie

Books
My Grandmother's Hands: Racialized Trauma and the Pathway to Mending Our Hearts and Bodies by Resmaa Menakem

Black Fatigue by Mary Frances Winters

The Color of Law – A Forgotten History of How Our Government Segregated America by Richard Rothstein

The Racial Healing Handbook by Annelise Singh

An Indigenous Peoples' History of the United States by Roxanne Dunbar-Ortiz

Lies My Teacher Told Me by James Lowen

A People's History of the United States by Howard Zinn

Caste by Isabel Wilkerson

Children's Books with a Native American or Indigenous Focus
We Are Still Here!: Native American Truths Everyone Should Know by Traci Sorrell

Fry Bread: A Native American Family Story by Kevin Noble Maillard

We Are Water Protectors by Carole Lindstrom and Michaela Goade

Jingle Dancer by Cynthia Leitich Smith and Ying Hwa-Hu

Stolen Words by Melanie Florence and Gabrielle Grimard

Young Adult Books with a Native American or Indigenous focus
Firekeeper's Daughter by Angeline Boulley

Chapter 5
Books
Raising White Kids by Jennifer Harvey

The First R by Debra Van Ausdale and Joe Feagin

Cultivating Genius: An Equity Framework for Culturally and Historically Responsive Literacy by Gholdy Muhammad

CHILDREN'S BOOKS

Hues of You: An Activity Book for Learning About the Skin You Are In by Lucretia Carter Berry

All the Colors We Are/Todos los colores de nuestra piel: The Story of How We Get Our Skin Color/La historia de por qué tenemos diferentes colores de piel by Katie Kissinger

The Colors of Us by Karen Katz

Shades of People by Shelley Rotner and Sheila M. Kelly

Skin Again by bell hooks and Chris Raschka

The Skin You Live In by Michael Tyler and David Lee Csicsko

Addy: An American Girl (American Girl Collection) by Connie Porter

Who Was/Is? Series about historical and current figures

M Is for Melanin: A Celebration of the Black Child by Tiffany Rose

ONLINE

b.Kids "Let's Learn About" by Brownicity.com, https://join.brownicity.com/courses/

BOOK DIVERSITY RESOURCES

Cooperative Children's Book Center

https://ccbc.education.wisc.edu/literature-resources/ccbc-diversity-statistics/

Leeandlow.com (BIPOC owned Book Company)
https://www.leeandlow.com/
The Brown Bookshelf
https://thebrownbookshelf.com/
We Need Diverse Books
https://diversebooks.org/
Zinn Education Project
https://www.zinnedproject.org/
Learning for Justice
https://www.learningforjustice.org/
Rethinking Schools
https://rethinkingschools.org/
Facing History and Ourselves
https://www.facinghistory.org/
Disrupt Texts
https://disrupttexts.org/

EVENT RESOURCES LISTED IN THE CHAPTER
Racial Equity Institute's Dismantling Racism. https://www.racial-equityinstitute.com/

Race – Are We So Different. National Science Foundation. https://www.nsf.gov/

Point Made Learning's *I'm Not Racist Am I?* *https://pointmadelearning.com/programs-and-services/film-screenings/im-not-racist-am-i/*

Chapter 6
WEBSITES
National Council of Teachers of English https://ncte.org/blog/2019/04/decolonizing-the-classroom/

Learning for Justice https://www.learningforjustice.org/

SOCIAL MEDIA ACCOUNTS
Brownicity
Teaching for Justice
Abolitionist Teaching Network
The Conscious Kid
Embrace Race
WE ARE
The Zinn Project
Education for Liberation

Chapter 7
TED TALK
Cultivating Seeds of Curiosity by Tehia Starker Glass https://www.youtube.com/watch?v=BUfuqp1PnIQ

BOOKS
Not Light, but Fire by Matthew Kay

The Latinization of U.S. Schools: Successful Teaching and Learning in Shifting Cultural Contexts by J. Irizarry

Ethnic Identity: Formation and Transmission Among Hispanics and Other Minorities edited by M. E. Bernal and G. P. Knight

CHILDREN'S BOOKS
Hues of You – An Activity Book for Learning About the Skin You Are In by Lucretia Berry

CHILDREN'S DIGITAL RESOURCE
"Let's Learn About" by Brownicity.com, https://join.brownicity.com/courses/b-kids

WEBSITES
Brownicity, https://brownicity.com/
EmbraceRace, https://www.embracerace.org/
Facing History & Ourselves, https://www.facinghistory.org/
Learning for Justice, https://www.learningforjustice.org/
Race – Are We So Different. National Science Foundation. https://www.nsf.gov/
Racial Equity Institute's Dismantling Racism, https://www.racialequityinstitute.com/
Abolitionist Teaching Network, https://abolitionistteachingnetwork.org/
Education for Liberation Network, https://www.edliberation.org/

Chapter 8
WEBSITES
"A Letter to White Teachers of My Black Children," by Afrika Afeni Mills,
https://www.teachingwhilewhite.org/blog/2019/6/21/a-letter-to-white-teachers-of-my-black-children
Zinn Education Project
https://www.zinnedproject.org/
Learning for Justice
https://www.learningforjustice.org/
Rethinking Schools
https://rethinkingschools.org/
Facing History and Ourselves
https://www.facinghistory.org/

Index